FOUR GREAT RELIGIONS

FOUR GREAT RELIGIONS

Four Lectures

Delivered on the Twenty-first Anniversary of the Theosophical Society, at Adyar, Madras

ANNIE BESANT

GYAN

Published by

Gyan Publishing House
5, Ansari Road
Daryaganj, New Delhi-110002
Phone: 011-47034999, 9811692060
E-mail: books@gyanbooks.com

Distribution Network
gyanbooks.com
India, USA, Canada, UK, Australia, France

ISBN: 978-81-212-9304-4 (PB)
First Published, 1897

2nd Impression 2023

Printed at: Gyan Press, Delhi.

FOUR GREAT RELIGIONS

Author: ANNIE BESANT

FOUR GREAT RELIGIONS

Four Lectures

Delivered on the Twenty-first Anniversary of the Theosophical Society, at Adyar, Madras

BY

ANNIE BESANT

Fellow of the Theosophical Society

LONDON
THEOSOPHICAL PUBLISHING SOCIETY
26 Charing Cross, S. W.
NEW YORK: THEOSOPHICAL PUBLISHING SOCIETY
65 Fifth Avenue
BENARES: THEOSOPHICAL PUBLISHING SOCIETY

1897

CONTENTS.

FOUR GREAT RELIGIONS.

FOREWORD.

THE following lectures do not pretend to be anything more than popular expositions of four great faiths, and are intended for the ordinary reader rather than for the student. Delivered to audiences composed almost entirely of Hindus, with only a sprinkling of Zoroastrians and Christians, they rather take for granted a knowledge of Sanskrit terms; so notes have been added where obscurity might arise from their use. They are intended to help members of each of the four religions to recognize the value and beauty of the three faiths which are not their own, and to demonstrate their underlying unity. In the lecture on Buddhism I had especially in mind the misconceptions which shut the Lord Buddha out from the hearts of His countrymen, and strove to remove them by quotations from the received Scriptures containing the authoritative records of His own words. For indeed I know of no greater service that could be rendered to religion than to draw together again these sundered faiths, which almost divide between them the Eastern world. Mother and daughter they are, and family feuds are proverbially bitter; yet might the quarrel be healed, if the desire for amity reigned on both sides. Less deeply rooted, but more keen, was the antagonism to Christianity, exasperated by the ignorant and often coarse and abusive attacks levelled by the lower class of missionaries against the venerable faith held by nearly all my hearers. Yet they listened respectfully and after a while sympathetically to the exposition of the faith so young in comparison with their own, and finally recognized that it also was a great religion, and was not really alien from Hinduism. I can wish these lectures no better fate than that they may act as a message of peace to the hearts of their readers, as they evidently did to the hearts of their hearers.

The general principles underlying these lectures are the following: Each religion is looked at in the light of occult knowledge, both as regards its history and its teachings. While not despising the conclusions arrived at by the patient and admirable work of European scholars, I have unhesitatingly flung them aside where they conflict with important facts preserved in occult history, whether in those imperishable records where all the past is still to be found in living pictures, or in ancient documents carefully stored up by Initiates and not wholly inaccessible. Especially is this the case with regard to the ages of Hinduism and Zoroastrianism, touching which modern scholarship is ludicrously astray. That scholarship, however, will regard the occult view as being, in its turn, grotesquely wrong. Be it so. Occultism can wait to be justified by discoveries, as so many of its much-ridiculed statements as to antiquity have already been; the earth is a faithful guardian, and as the archæologist uncovers the cities buried in her bosom many an unexpected witness will be found to justify the antiquity that is claimed.

Secondly, each religion is treated as coming from the one great Brotherhood which is the steward and custodian of spiritual knowledge. Each is treated as an expression, by some member or messenger of that Brotherhood of the eternal spiritual truths, an expression suited to the needs of the time at which it was made, and of the dawning civilization that it was intended to mould and to guide in its evolution. Each religion has its own mission in the world, is suited to the nations to whom it is given, and to the type of civilization it is to permeate, bringing it into line with the general evolution of the human family. The failure to see this leads to unjust criticism, for an ideally perfect religion would not be suitable to imperfect and partially evolved men, and environment must always be considered by the Wise when They plant a new slip of the ancient tree of wisdom.

Thirdly, an attempt is made to distinguish the essential from the non-essential in each religion, and to treat chiefly the former. For every religion in the course of time suffers from accretions due to ignorance—not to wisdom; to blindness—not to vision.

Within the brief compass of these lectures, it was not possible to distinguish in detail, nor to point out, all the numerous non-essentials. But the following tests may be used by any one who desires to guide himself practically in discriminating between the permanent and the transitory elements in any religion. Is it ancient, to be found in the ancient Scriptures? Has it the authority of the Founder of the religion, or of the Sages to whom the formulation of the particular religion is due? Is it universal, found under some form in all religions? As regards spiritual truths, any one of these tests is sufficient. As to smaller matters, matters of rites and ceremonies, observances and customs, the use or disuse of any particular practice, we may ask as to each: Is it laid down or recommended in the ancient Scriptures, by the Founder or His immediate disciples? Can its usefulness be explained or verified by those in whom occult training has developed the inner faculties which make the invisible world a region they know by their own experience? If a custom be of modern growth, with only a century, or two or three centuries, behind it, if it be local, not found in any ancient Scripture, nor justified by occult knowledge, then—however helpful it may be found by an individual in his spiritual life—it should not be imposed on any member of a particular religion as binding on him as a part of that religion, nor should a man be looked at askance for non-compliance with it. This fact especially needs enforcement in India, where customs that are entirely local, or very modern, are apt to be identified with Hinduism in the minds of their followers, and any Hindus who do not accept them are looked upon as somewhat inferior, even as unorthodox. Such customs, even if much valued and found useful by their adherents, should not be considered as generally binding, and should fall into the class of non-essentials. It has been well said that while in things essential there should be unity, in things non-essential there should be liberty, and in all things there should be charity. Were that wise rule followed by each, we should hear less of the religious antagonisms and sectarian disputes that bring shame on the very word "religion." That which ought to unite has been the ever-springing source of division, until many have impatiently shaken off all religion as being man's worst enemy, the introducer everywhere of strife and hatred.

May this little book, sent out with reverence for all religions that purify man's life, elevate his emotions and comfort him in sorrow, be a message of peace, and not a stirring-up of strife; for I have striven to sketch each religion in its best, its purest, and most occult form, and each as though I belonged to it and were preaching it as my own. To the Theosophist "nothing that is human is foreign," and he has only reverent sympathy for every expression of man's longing after God. He seeks to understand all, to convert none, and in offering to share the knowledge with which he has been intrusted, he hopes to deepen every man's faith by adding to his faith knowledge, and by unveiling the common foundation which supports all religions.

ANNIE BESANT.

Owing to pressure of time many quotations, supporting the positions taken, were either summarized or omitted in the spoken lectures. They have been inserted in their proper places, together with a few points that were in the original notes but were also omitted for lack of time.

ADYAR, *January 3d, 1897.*

HINDUISM.

Never, my brothers, since I have stood on the platform in order to put forth thoughts on religion and on philosophy, have I felt the difficulty of the task that is undertaken more than I feel it on this occasion. The mere fact of dealing with four great religions, each compressed into a single lecture, is by itself enough to appall the most audacious of speakers; and when you consider that with the feelings of your hearers these religious matters are intimately bound up, that one is going down to the very roots of the human heart, that in taking faith after faith one is dealing with those matters which ought to have united men, but as a matter of fact have very largely divided them, then you may appreciate the hesitation that I feel in trying in any sense to grapple with a task so great. A religion can only be understood by sympathy; a religion can only be expounded by the speaker placing himself, for the time being, in the heart of that religion and showing it forth as it would appear to its most devoted and learned adherents; and this I am to try to do with four of those great religions that have moulded the civilizations of men, that have colored the thoughts and comforted the hearts of the vast majority of the human race.

The first of the great religions with which I am to deal is that known sometimes under the name of Hinduism, sometimes under the name of Brâhmanism, a religion which is the religion of the majority in this country and which had its cradle in the northern part of this land. Let me begin by reminding you that this race, the Áryan race, is the fifth in the course of human evolution, and that in the case of this race, as in the case of the one that went before it, a definite plan was followed in its formation and its training. From the flower of the fourth race, that preceded it, at a time so distant that modern science would only jeer at it if given, families were chosen out by the Manu to form the forthcoming race, were separated from the earlier humanity, segregated, and placed apart, and, for an immense period of time, trained, guided, and educated under the immediate direction of the Manu and the great Initiates who surrounded Him to help Him in His mighty task. Thus the characteristics of the new race were impressed on the flower of the old. When that early task was over, the race was planted in what we may call its cradle-land. In this way the Áryan race was formed, was trained, and had its own characteristics implanted in it; the first family of its stock, from which others were later to spring—that which in modern times we speak of as Hindu, but that always in the early days was called Áryan—that was settled in the North of India in the district known as Áryâvarta, and there gradually evolved along definite lines laid down for it by its

Manu and by the Initiates who surrounded Him. In this case we find that the model for the whole race is definitely imprinted on its first family; that which ought to be perfectly reproduced is here perfectly expressed, and the perfection of the expression is due to those on whom this early impression is made. For, looking backward in the light of occult knowledge on those beginnings, we find that the souls that were incarnated in this beginning of the Áryan race were souls of many different types. The Manu at the head of all, the ruler and the legislator; then the Initiates round Him, the teachers and guides of the people—the Rishis of ancient India; below them a large number of souls coming into incarnation, who had already attained a high stage of moral, intellectual, and spiritual development in previous stages of evolution, and even in previous worlds; below them younger souls, who had still much evolution behind them; and lastly a number of souls who had had a very brief time of evolution, comparatively speaking, who had passed through the fourth race and were the most successful members of that great division of humanity. So that you had a very various people, a people who could well take the impress of an all-embracing religion, philosophy, science, and polity, and serve as a model, handing down to their more untrained successors who should follow them this example of what an Áryan, a fifth-race nation, ought to be. It was fitted to be the custodian of the polity, of the philosophy, of the sciences, of the exoteric religion, and to mark out once for all what ought to be the typical development of the Áryan race.

Now we find, as we study the religion given to the ancient people, that it includes a training for the whole nature of man at the various stages of his evolution, and that it guides him not only in his spiritual and intellectual life, but also in all his relations with his fellow-men in the life of the nation and of the family. The whole civilization is religious, and there is nothing in human life regarded as "secular" or as "profane." The things which are looked on by other peoples as outside the scope of religion are the very things as to which Hinduism has always most rigidly demanded orthodoxy. The intellect has been encouraged to exert itself freely, as witness the schools of thought comprised under the all-embracing "Hinduism;" but right conduct as it affects the social fabric has ever been rigidly enforced. Freedom in opinion, but orthodoxy in life, have been characteristic of Hinduism throughout its long evolution; hence the vast range and diversity of its philosophies, and the stability of its social fabric and its family life. Hence too it has been looked on as the most burdensome of religions, for most people care much for liberty of action and little (except theoretically) for liberty of thought. A Hindu may think as he will about God—as one with the universe, separate from the universe, or may even exclude Him entirely—and yet be orthodox; but he must not intermarry with another caste, nor eat polluted food.

Our subject falls naturally into three divisions: (1) the spiritual truths, with their later intellectual presentations; these are given in the Vedas and in the Upanishads which are an integral portion of them. We have in the Vedas a complete presentment of spiritual truth, not fully expressed but implicitly contained, so that it is written that Brahman is concealed in the Upanishads as the Upanishads are concealed in the Vedas. Gradually this was to be expressed in the course of evolution; a perfect whole was given to be unfolded as time went on. This was the higher Vidyâ,[1] the knowledge of Brahman, and the lesser Vidyâ was comprised in the Vedângaṣ,[2] the sixty-four sciences which codified the knowledge of nature and the methods of gaining knowledge, a mine of gold from which might now be digged out scientific lore that would set the modern world a-wondering.

Then comes (2) the exoteric cult, detailed and wonderfully minute in its delineation of nature and of a man's relation thereto, with the Purânas as its popular expression, with the Ordinances linking it to the outer social and family conduct. Later on, we find book after book, like the Râmâyana, and the Mahâbhârata, and in much later times there are fresh expressions of their truths in some of the dramas, such as those of Kalidâsa. Here for the people at large, for the mass of the population, there are the outer teachings which are gradually to train them to the understanding of the hidden and spiritual truths.

[1] Knowledge.

[2] Literally "limbs of the Vedas."

You will never understand Hinduism unless you realize that it was a system given by occultists, by Rishis, to whom the invisible world was a matter of knowledge; that it was intended to train the people gradually into a knowledge of it, by their following of a system based on the facts of the invisible. You must realize this foundation of the religion and then you can trace it out in all its varying parts. Then you will understand why, as already said, the intellect has always been left free, bounded only by the Vedas, left free to infer from the Vedas whatever it might logically deduce from their many-faced and profound wisdom, while outer conduct was so rigidly guarded. By a man's thoughts a man evolves, and the thoughts of others are powerful factors in the evolution of each; the more varied they are, the more openings do they make through which the sun of truth can shine. Varieties of opinion about God are valuable, not mischievous, because each opinion by itself expresses so small a fragment of the mighty truth, and the totality of opinions gives a fuller presentation than could otherwise be gained. But conduct covers all man's relations to external nature, visible and invisible, and according to his conduct harmony or discord accrues. The exoteric cult was intended to make a harmonious concord between man and his surroundings, and was imposed by authority because the people were not capable of assimilating the knowledge on which it was based. In their later evolution, when knowledge was acquired by Yoga, the outer obligations fell away, for harmony then needed no authority for its production; the man, united to the law, became a law unto himself. Here comes in (3)-the Science of Yoga,[1] through which spiritual truths can alone be fully realized, by the gradual unfolding of the inner faculties which enable man to study the invisible world directly, by the expansion of his consciousness to embrace wider and subtler ranges of being. The truths given in the Vedas were to be realized by Yoga, but its methods are nowhere fully stated, and to this end was the Guru instituted, that he might teach the worthy pupil to tread this difficult path, sharp as the edge of a razor.

We shall take these three divisions in order. First, we shall look at the spiritual truths which are expressed in the Vedas, with the aspects of these expounded in the systems of philosophy—partial because intellectual, complementary not antagonistic; not one of them expressing the whole of the truth, but each expressing as much as the intellect is able to put logically together under a single system. Then we shall study the exoteric cult in its principles, in its details, showing the bearing of the whole on the social and family life. Lastly we shall realize that a true knowledge of spiritual truths can only be obtained by Yoga, that there is a science of the soul which is taught by the Guru, and which enables a man step by step to rise to the highest spiritual wisdom. You see how vast an area of ground we have to cover; you see how this morning, in so short a time, we have to traverse this vast field of study, and you

[1] Union with the Self.

will pardon me if, in passing swiftly from point to point, I leave much detail utterly unexpressed, because I am speaking with the tongue, not by mind to mind, and am limited by that illusion of time under which all our intellectual processes here must be carried on.

I begin with a brief exposition of the fundamental spiritual and philosophical truths on which the whole of Hinduism is based, the understanding of which perfectly means that man has reached his goal. Let us glance at the beginning of the universe, the commencement of manifestation, when Brahman, the Self of the universe, manifests Himself in order that the universe may be. It is written: "When He is manifest, all is manifested after Him; by His manifestation this all becomes manifest."[1] How He comes into manifestation we know not, but we are told that it is by an act of sacrifice: "Om! the dawn in truth is the head of the sacrificial horse."[2] Occult wisdom teaches that this act of sacrifice is the Self-limitation of Brahman, His circumscribing of Himself by Mâyâ, *i.e.*, by Avidyâ.[3] Without this no universe could be manifest, since limitation is necessary to variety, and each thing is enveloped in Avidyâ; that is, is limited, is shut out from being all else, from

[1] *Mundakopanishad*, II., ii., 10.

[2] *Brihadâranyakopanishad*, I., i., 1.

[3] Mâyâ is illusion, all that is changing, transitory, in contrast to the permanent Reality, the One Life. Therefore it is the root of matter, matter being that which takes form and adapts itself to the impulses of the life it clothes. Avidyâ, absence of knowledge, is another name for it.

being perfect knowledge. With Brahman the manifested universe begins; He is the Source, the Fount, the one Self, and the one Breath of the universe; outside Him is nothing that is manifest; outside Him there is no life, no thought, no mind; manifesting in His three-fold attributes, He is Sat, Chit, Ánanda, and from Him all qualities come forth. He enfolds these in one, the First, the Cause of all. That Brahman, that mighty one, the Self of the universe, is described in a passage of wonderful beauty and sublimity in the *Shvetâshvataropanishad*, and I choose this because in a shloka quickly following after this description the hint of something beyond even the manifested Brahman is given. You may remember the passage, which I must needs translate into the less poetical, less beautiful, and less perfect language which I am obliged to employ, but even in the modern tongue the marvellous beauty of the original shines forth: "When there is no darkness, neither day nor night, neither being nor non-being, there is Shiva even alone. He is indestructible. He is to be adored by Savitri, from Him alone comes forth the ancient wisdom. Not above, nor below, nor in the midst can He be comprehended, nor is there any similitude for Him whose name is infinite glory. Not by the sight is established His form: none beholds Him by the eye. Those who knew Him by the heart and the mind, dwelling in the heart, become immortal."[1] Such is the description of Brahman, the manifested, the Cause of the universe. Two shlocas

[1] *Op. cit.*, iv., 18, 19, 20.

follow, and then the succeeding chapter opens with the declaration that in Parabrahman, the supreme Brahman, "Vidyâ and Avidyâ exist unmanifest."[1] Or we may translate: "Ishvara and Mâyâ[2] exist unmanifest." What that means we know not, what that would signify we cannot say. No human faculties may cognize the unconditioned; no human tongue can express THAT which is beyond this all. Only we know that all comes forth from THAT; THAT is everything, though no words implying difference—and all words imply difference—may describe THAT; in THAT Sat, Chit, and Ánanda have their root in unity, the One without a second; in THAT, Unknown and Unknowable, all is, but is in a way we cannot understand. For to us existence means difference, and in THAT difference there is none.

Then, coming to the manifested universe, where some knowledge is possible to us, we learn that the manifestation of Brahman is gradual and not sudden, and that all comes forth from Him not at once but slowly; from the concealed gradually comes forth the manifest; from the hidden comes forth the revealed. Phrase after phrase is used to show you that everything comes forth from and is Himself, but that He is hidden beneath the phenomena, beneath Name and Form. As salt in the water in which it is dissolved,[3] as fire in the wood before the

[1] *Ibid*, v., 1.

[2] Ishvara, the Lord, Brahman as the source of the universe and its guiding power. Mâyâ see *ante*.

[3] *Chhândogyopanishad*, VI., xiv.

fire-sticks are rubbed together, as butter in the milk that is brought forth by churning,[1] as cream in clarified butter,[2] so is Brahman concealed as the Self of every creature. Stage after stage the marvels of His manifestation; stage by stage the might of His unfolding; His quality of Sat, of pure existence, comes forth in the unmoving creation, in the mineral kingdom as we call it, where existence only can be said to be shown; Chit and Ánanda are there concealed, and only Sat is manifest. Then in the vegetable world the unfolding life shows us the beginning of pleasure and pain, the germ which develops into Ánanda in the later stages of evolution; and in the animal world there is shown forth also the germ of Chit, which is to have its later and fuller evolution; and in man the germs are all partially manifested of Sat, Chit, and Ánanda, until at the end of his evolution Sat, Chit, and Ánanda are perfectly developed in him. Then he is Brahman, he has become one.

All this is wrought out by the slow course of evolution, by birth after birth, by death after death, by that wheel of births and deaths which turns unceasingly in the three worlds. The lowest world, the world of our waking consciousness, is Bhurloka; there man is born in the physical body, there he gathers experience by coming into contact with material objects; then through the gateway of death he passes into the next world, Bhuvarloka, and in a body suited to that world he works out a part of the

[1] *Shvetâshvatarop.*, i., 14–19. [2] *Ibid.*, iv., 16.

experience made upon the earth; then in a third body, ascending to Svargaloka, he works out the fruits of others of his earthly experiences.[1] From Svargaloka he returns again through Bhuvarloka to the gateway of birth, to Bhurloka, there to begin again his learning, the fruits of which he assimilates in the other worlds. Thus ordinary human evolution is in the three worlds—as we are constantly told.

To this wheel man is bound by desire, by the thirst for sentient existence, which in his ignorance he identifies at first with the life of the body. "This Purusha [inner man] has the nature of desire. As is his desire so is his resolve; as is his resolve so is his work; as is his work, so is his reward. . . . He who is attached obtains by means of work the object to which his mind, as the cause, is attached. Having arrived at the last (effect) [in Svarga] of the work which he here performs, he comes from that world again to this world in consequence of work. Thus he who desires (wanders from world to world) . . . . When all desires dwelling in the heart have been abandoned, then the mortal becomes immortal."[2] Ceasing to identify himself with the body, he next identifies himself with the mind, and then merely lives for a longer time in Svarga, still bound by desire. Freedom from rebirth only comes when desire is dead for anything the three worlds have to give.

[1] This earth, the astral world, devachan.

[2] *Brihadâranyakopanishad*, IV., iv., 5-7.

Next, all this evolution proceeds under the law of causation, each cause working out its due effect. This is the law of Karma, that returns to every man exactly the result of his sowing. He sows his Karma in the world of matter, of physical matter, he reaps it partially in the other two worlds and there assimilates the results of his thinking; then he returns to earth, the creature of his own making, to work out Karma belonging to this earth; so he grows, life after life, being "a creature of reflection; what he reflects on in this life he becomes the same hereafter."[1] In this way he climbs from stage to stage with ever-expanding consciousness, sheath after sheath developing within him, and each one a vehicle of consciousness. As he develops, he expands his consciousness to embrace one world after another—the stages of consciousness corresponding to those three worlds being the states of Jagrat, Svapna, and Sushupti.[2] Consciousness expands, embracing each world in turn until man is the master and sovereign where at first he was the child and the student. Then, rising yet higher, he escapes from the wheel of births and deaths; he passes from the

[1] *Chhândogyopanishad*, III., xiv., 1.

[2] Consciousness is a unit, but it may work in the Jagrat state, *i.e.*, in the physical body in Bhurloka; or in the Svapna state, *i.e.*, in the astral body in Bhuvarloka; or in the Sushupti state, *i.e.*, in the mental body in Svargaloka. Hence Jagrat is called the waking consciousness, Svapna the dream-consciousness, and Sushupti the dreamless-sleep-consciousness. The English names are misleading unless the facts are understood.

body of the moon,[1] as it is technically called, into the body of the sun,[2] and when this is completely mastered he comes back no more to enforced birth. Rising to the Turîya state, he attains the Self, clad only in the Ânandamayakosha.[3] Having definitely unified his consciousness to that point, he is beyond the three worlds and their revolving wheel. He can pass into, expand into, the Nirvânic consciousness, the all-embracing, the divine. Jîvâtmâ—thrown forth at first in the uttermost ignorance, enveloped in Avidyâ, with all its powers germinal, in latency not in activity—is enwrapped in sheath after sheath of matter in order that, through the sheaths, it may come into contact with all the regions of the universe, that in each it may, by these contacts, bring forth into manifestation the powers belonging to that region at first latent in itself, until at last all the powers are developed, the sheaths are purified, Avidyâ is transcended, and man knows that the Self of the universe and his own Self are one; he finds his goal, he becomes Brahman; that which he ever was potentially he becomes actively and in realization.

Such, roughly sketched, are the essentials of that mighty philosophy of Hinduism by which man is taught something of the spiritual truths that underlie evolution. All this will be done by humanity life after life. But what all men will do in the course of countless ages a man may do, if he will, by greater effort, by intenser exertion, by means of

[1] The astral and mental bodies. [2] The causal body.
[3] The bliss-body.

that science of Yoga which trains the soul more swiftly than the ordinary evolution. Evolution is but the will of Íshvara showing itself in the manifested universe; borne on the bosom of evolution, humanity is carried onward to its goal. But the strong swimmer may reach the goal more swiftly than a floating straw; by Yoga a man may finish his journey while yet the mass of humanity are floating slowly along with the current of evolution. This we shall see in the third division of our subject.

Attempts to bring down this wonderful thought to the region of intellect have given birth to the six great schools of Indian Philosophy, with all their countless modifications. We descend from the spiritual region into the intellectual, from that world where all is clear to the purified vision into the world where limitations have their way—and language is the worst limitation of all, yet every philosopher must write, must express himself, in articulate form. Yet how shall the Unspeakable be uttered, how shall Brahman be put in intellectual terms? One mark is common to all the schools and may be said to be written above their portals: "Until a man is able to roll up the âkâsha like leather, there will be no end of misery except by the knowledge of God."[1] Every school of Hindu philosophy seeks liberation, liberation from the limits of painful existence, from the miseries of birth and death. All admit that the divine knowledge, Brahma Vidyâ, is wanted for the escape, but they differ in the way they express

[1] *Shvetâshvataropanishad*, vi., 20.

their goal, in the methods they severally employ to reach it. Let us take them for a moment one by one—it is all I can do—just that you may realize the vast work intellect has done in trying to expound spiritual truths. They fall readily into three pairs, characterized by their fundamental view of the universe and by their way of proof. First we have those founded on the atomic theory, the two schools known as the Nyâya of Gotama and the Vaisheshika of Kanâda, which have also very much in common in their methods of research. They seek knowledge by way of inference, by logical process, dividing everything into categories, considering the nature of proof, the nature of inference, the very essence as it were of the mind, worked out in full details, based on the atomic theory and developed along the lines of pure reason. They remain as monuments of pure intellection, remarkable not only for the perfection with which the reasoning is conducted, but also for the training they give to the human mind; the nature of things is sought into, and in order that error may be avoided there is the keenest analysis of the tools by which that investigation is to be made. Then you come to the two schools which are built on the duality of the manifested universe, on the co-eternity in it of the two fundamentals, never disjoined, ever interworking, a cosmogony of the most logical coherence being worked out in linked succession. These are the Sânkhya of Kapila, sometimes called the atheistic Sânkhya, because it does not go behind the dual manifestation, and the Yoga of Patanjali, or the theistic Sânkhya. In the first, the fundamental duality of the manifested universe is the starting-point. Purusha, Spirit, or rather the multitude of individual Purushas, is regarded as eternal, and Prakriti, matter, is regarded as co-eternal with them. Prakriti is threefold, showing Sattva, Rajas, and Tamas as its three gunas,[1] and is full of activities, but it is aimless and can do nothing save as clothing Purusha. Hence the favorite simile, that Purusha is like a lame man with effective eyes carried on the shoulders of a blind man with effective legs; the two together can walk and avoid stumbling into pitfalls. Then follows the working out of the whole manifested universe, under the heads of twenty-five tattvas or principles, as we may call them, deduced with keen insight, with logical precision, with the most careful observation of facts, so that, taken as a cosmogony limited to the manifested universe, the Sânkhya may be said to ever hold its own. The Yoga of Patanjali accents the Sânkhya cosmogony as it stands, but adds to it the twenty-sixth tattva, Íshvara, the deity to be worshipped. For Patanjali truly said that without a form the mind could not concentrate itself in meditation, and he sought knowledge not by investigation into the universe along the Sânkhya lines, but by the suppression of the modifications of the thinking principle; those modifications were regarded as the barrier between the thinker and the One that he sought; only when the mind

[1] Serenity, activity, inertia as its three qualities.

was one-pointed could man escape from this limitation.

Lastly, we have the two great Mimâmsa schools, the Purva Mimâmsa and the Uttara Mimâmsa. In the first, the system of Jaimani, we have rites, ceremonies, all that is the outer part of a man's religious life, dealt with and expounded with the utmost minuteness. The Uttara Mimâmsa is the Vedânta, the best known perhaps in the West of these six great Indian schools. This is divided into three sub-schools, the Dvaita, Vishishtadvaita, and the Advaita. They accept the Sânkhya cosmogony as to the course of the evolution of the manifested universe, but are not satisfied to stop where the Sânkhya stops. The Vedânta—the "end of the Vedas"—seeks the cause of the manifested universe, cannot rest content with an analysis that stops at Purusha and Prakriti. It is, in fact, the most splendid and philosophical expression of that ineradicable yearning of the human heart for God, which may be denied, distorted, thwarted, but ever rises from its seeming death, the eternal witness of something in man that is his innermost Self, his inalienable life, and that finds its noblest outcome in the triumph-cry of the Advaitin, "I am He!" when the long-sought under many veils is found, and Deity stands revealed as the very Self of man.

The three sub-schools of the Vedânta should be regarded as successive steps, rather than as antagonistic theories; all assert the Divine existence as the source of the universe, but the Dvaita teaching alleges an eternal division between God and man—they remain eternally distinct. The Vishishtadvaita goes a step further, asserting duality but merging it into a final unity. The Advaita insists on the fundamental unity, and is so intent on this that—dazzled by the darkness that is "excess of light"—it well-nigh loses sight of the universe, seeing only the One under the illusive forms. But when from intellectual disquisition he rises into devotion, the Advaita Vedântin also recognizes the manifestation of Brahman in the Gods, and where can we find such fervid overmastering intensity of rapt devotion as in the stotras to Shiva and to Durgâ of that chief of Advaita Vedântins, Shrî Shankarâchârya?

In the Advaita is the familiar teaching as to Mâyâ, the illusion-causing power of Divine Thought—the universe but the thought of the One without a second. All but Brahman is illusion, for it is limited, it is transient, it is ever-changing; the One that is permanent is the only Reality; all that changes is illusory, the manifestation is but a thought. Perhaps that idea, difficult to grasp, may be made clearer if we remember that the human mind can also by its thought impose illusions on another mind that is under its control. When a man is hypnotized he can be made to feel the resistance of a body, to see it, to hear it, to touch it and smell it, to have every record of the senses by which we guide our outer life complete, and yet there is nothing there but the thought of the hypnotizer, who is imposing all these sensations directly on the mind.

The moment the man is dehypnotized the illusion vanishes, and he knows nothing is there. Similarly, in this view, the universe is but God's thought expressed and dominating the whole—all forms are but thoughts of God; and when that is once realized the One is seen and the separation and the difference disappear. Sheath after sheath of Avidyâ is stripped from off the Self; sheath after sheath is pierced through by the eye of wisdom, until the seer declares that "In the highest golden sheath is spotless, partless Brahman, THAT, the true light of lights, known to the knowers of the Self."[1] Or yet man has known it, he wanders about in the universe of forms, but that which really attracts him in every form is not the phenomenal appearance but the Self which shines within it. We love forms because the Self is in them; we are attracted by forms because a broken ray of the light of the Self shines through. As the child sees the pebble shining on the road after rain, and goes to pick up the shining stone, attracted not by the dull bit of earth but by the light of the sun which is reflected from it, so do all men—aye! even in their vices—deluded by outer appearance, follow but the broken light of the Self. That is what they are groping after, and in their blindness they fail to understand, they do not realize. All persons too are loved for the Self within them. "Not for the sake of the wife the wife is dear, but for the sake of the Self the wife is dear; not for the sake of the husband is the husband dear, but for the

[1] *Mundakopanishad*, II., ii., 9.

sake of the Self is the husband dear;" and so on with one thing after another in the manifested universe, until at last we say: "Not for the sake of the Gods the Gods are dear, but for the sake of the Self the Gods are dear."[1] Thus Man rises from stage to stage, ever coming nearer to the Self; thus it is that first he realizes division—"I am I, Thou art Thou; Thou art to be adored, Thou art to be worshipped; I am thy Bhakta, Thy devotee." Coming nearer and nearer to the vision of light, there comes a dawning sense of likeness, the lover and the beloved cannot be really twain; until at last, with love made perfect and wisdom no longer stained by ignorance, the lover and the beloved merge in one, "I am He!" and there is unity where duality had reigned.

From this you may probably see why it was that in the old days the teaching of the Vedânta was not given to the world at large. The path of the unmanifested, says Shrî Krishna, "is hard for the embodied to reach."[2] Through the embodied we rise to the unembodied, through forms to the formless. Therefore Shrî Shankarâchârya laid it down as a preparation for learning the Advaita that the man should evolve in himself certain qualifications, and until those were evolved the Advaita was never taught. How wise and necessary this restriction we can appreciate who see the evil use to which this noble teaching is put to-day by men with senses uncontrolled and minds untrained.

[1] *Brihadâranyopanishad*, IV., v., 6.

[2] *Bhagavad Gîtâ*, xii., 5.

We now pass from those great philosophic systems, dealt with so terribly baldly, to the exoteric cult, which was intended to train, to evolve, to educate the soul, until rising from step to step it was ready to pass into the hands of the Guru and receive its final initiations.

The first thing that strikes us in the exoteric religion is its all-embracing character, its infinitely varied adaptations to the infinitely varied needs of man. And this, because it presents the external universe from the occult standpoint and because that universe at every point touches each soul at the successive stages of its long evolution. For the very poorest, the lowest, the meanest, the most ignorant, there was something in the faith; for the highest, the most intellectual, the most spiritually advanced, there was still teaching in Hinduism. That is one of its distinguishing characteristics, that it has teaching for the most ignorant and for the most wise, embracing them all within the same fold of religion.

The exoteric cult was based on a knowledge of nature—occult knowledge; not the knowledge that science obtains by studying phenomena, that is, the outer appearances; but the knowledge that springs from studying the inner life, that is, the mind of which the outer phenomena are the expressions. There you have the fundamental difference between occult and physical science. The one looks at the outer appearance, the other looks at the life which is manifesting itself through the form. Based, then, on facts of the invisible world, the whole teaching of it is the expression of invisible nature, of nature not as matter and energy but as living intelligences, not as "blind" or "dead" matter and unconscious force, but as living consciousnesses expressing themselves through matter and through energy. Their life is really the energy, consciousness being of the essence of life; forms are matter veiling the life, matter taking shape from the living consciousness within it. On this profound truth, that there is nothing in the universe that is not living, and that all forms are the expressions in denser or subtler matter of the thoughts of living intelligences, the exoteric cult of Hinduism is based. It was intended, as before said, to bring man, however ignorant he might be, into harmony with his visible and invisible environment; it taught him to use rites, ceremonies, formulæ (mantras), every one of which was designed to produce definite results in the invisible world; to preserve unbroken the interdependent links of elemental, mineral, vegetable, animal, human, lives; to keep turning in harmonious rhythm the wheel of life in the three worlds, supporting in mutual service the minerals, vegetables, animals and men of the physical world, the Devatas of the astral world, the Devas of the mind-world, establishing that system of reciprocal sacrifice to which Shrî Krishna alluded when He said: "With this nourish ye the Gods, and may the Gods nourish you; thus nourishing one another, ye shall reap the supremest good. For, nourished by sacrifice, the Gods shall bestow on you the enjoyments you desire."[1] That which the occultist does by knowledge and by will-power, ignorant men were taught to do in their little measure by rites and ceremonies, so contributing their small share to the general harmonious working of the whole.

The Sat-Chit-Ánanda of the philosopher, of the spiritual mystic, is expressed in the concrete form of the Trimûrti[2]—Brahmâ, Vishnu, Shiva. There we have in concrete forms adapted for worship the threefold Brahman who is the Cause of the universe; His three aspects shown in their separate manifestation, in order that they may be understood a little better by the limited intelligences of men. The creative aspect is shown forth in Brahmâ, by whose tapas, or meditation, all things are produced; He expresses the universal mind, the divine Chit. The life which is in everything, the life which permeates, which sustains, the infinite support, the foundation of the universe, that without which the universe could not be maintained, which is present in everything, in every atom of that universe, is Vishnu, the All-Pervader, the sustaining life of God; He, the dual, is the aspect of Ánanda, of bliss. And then, more hidden and mysterious in many ways, He who is sometimes called the Destroyer but is rather the Regenerator, He who is living Fire, the Lord of the burning ground, whose fire comes down to burn up every form when its usefulness is over, in order to

[1] *Bhagavad Gîtâ*, iii., 11, 12.
[2] Three images, the Trinity.

liberate the life that is within the form, that it may take higher expression and fuller manifestation—He, Mahâdeva, Maheshvara, is Sat, existence. Such is the great Trimûrti, the concrete aspects of the manifested God. Then coming downward from the Trimûrti we have the seven great "elements," each of which is the form-aspect of a mighty Intelligence, a God, of whom five only are at present manifest and two concealed. These five are Ákâsha, the form animated by Indra; Agni, fire, the form of Agni; Vâyu, Air, the form of Pavana; Ap, water, that of Varuna; Prithivi, earth, that of Kshiti.

You will never understand the wonderful perfection of the Hindu cult unless you can realize something of the life-side of the universe. These Gods of the elements—Indra, Agni, Pavana, Varuna, and Kshiti—these are real entities, great spiritual Intelligences, and each one of Them has His own region; each one of Them is Lord and sovereign Ruler of that particular element which is the expression of His nature, and below Him there are countless hosts of Devas and Devatas in ever-descending order, until you come down to the lowest manifestations of all on the physical plane, the lowest Devatas of Hinduism, who have to do with the absolute forming and building of the physical bodies of our physical world. Also you have to understand that while there are seven great regions in the universe[1]—of which we are concerned with five only—each one consisting of modifications of the element which is

[1] The seven planes of the Theosophist.

its root-material, each of these regions has also its seven subdivisions, and these subdivisions severally show the characteristics of the great regions. Borrowing an illustration from our revered teacher, H. P. Blavatsky, I may compare the seven regions of the universe to the seven colors of the solar spectrum; then imagine that, taking one color, say violet, this is analyzed into seven again, and is found to consist of violet-red, violet-orange, violet-yellow, violet-green, violet-blue, violet-indigo, violet-violet; each color of the spectrum there, but dominated by the violet shade: there you have an admirable picture of the way in which each God has His own region, and yet the other Gods are represented in it by modifications of the element of the ruling God, each subdivision being characterized by the attributes of one of the others. If, for instance, you take Fire, Agni is the ruling God, and is Fire in every region of the universe—electric fire, all flashings of light, light in the highest heaven as in lowest earth. These all come under His rule, are modes of His being, and condition it according to the region where the manifestation takes place, down to the physical fire that burns on the hearth, whose Devatas are animated by His life. Therefore Agni, the mighty, the self-shining, ruling in the fiery region, is yet chanted in the *Sama Veda* as "The Lord of the Homestead," for the household fire is also His and through it He works.

Then we come to men's relations with them, men's relations with the ascending hierarchies, going right up to the Trimûrti; these are set forth in order, with the rites, the ceremonies and the ıelig-ious duties connected with each at every stage; according to a man's intellectual and spiritual evolution is the grade of Deity to whom his worship should be paid. For those who are just awakening to the consciousness of mind and are feeling the first faint stirrings of devotion, some very simple form of God is given; otherwise they can understand nothing of what is meant by the very word "God." Hinduism gives them a concrete form, a concrete form of an exceedingly narrow kind at first; else it would only daze the dawning intellect, and confuse the dull feeling of devotion which otherwise might gradually develop. Would you talk to the laborer in his field, who knows nothing but his seed, his crops, his cattle, his hopes of rainfall and sunshine, his wife and his children—would you talk to him of the spotless, partless Brahman who is known to the knower of the Self? If you do he will stare at you blankly; you give him no object towards which his love can go out, towards which his devotion can find its way, round which the tiny tendrils of his heart can twine themselves, at present so weak and able to grasp so little. When a tender plant is shooting, you do not bring an enormous rock to that plant, expecting it to twine round it with its baby tendrils; but you take a slender twig, which is not too large for the tendril to twine around, by which the plant climbs, grows upwards, and by its aid becomes stronger and ever more able to grow. So, in the exoteric cult of Hinduism, the aspect presented of God is proportional to the ability of the worshipper—always a little above him, always a little higher than he is, always such as to draw out some feeling of love, of devotion, and of homage, and all that really goes to the One, no matter under what aspect that One may be seen. "A leaf, a flower, water, a fruit"[1] offered with pure heart, with sincere devotion, is accepted by Shrî Krishna Himself, as though offered unto Him. For "even devotees of other Gods who worship, full of faith, they also worship me, O son of Kuntî, though contrary to the ancient rule;"[2] much more then they who worship the lower Gods according to that ancient rule. And why not, since there is nothing "moving or unmoving that may exist bereft of me,"[3] and therefore the Lord is in the stone or the tree, and He is worshipped and not the mere outer form?

So is it, step by step, that the worshipper is led upwards as by a loving mother's hand. And if you want to have in a single scene the necessity for this limitation, go to the eleventh division of the *Bhagavad Gîtâ*, where Arjuna, not knowing what he asks, prays to see Shrî Krishna as the Lord of the Universe and not in His more limited form. Shrî Krishna grants his prayer, gives him the divine eye, since the eye of flesh cannot see God. And then He shines forth in splendor, like a thousand suns shining at once in the heavens, filling height and depth, stretching from east to west, from north to south,

[1] *Bhagavad Gîtâ*, ix., 26. [2] *Ibid.*, 23. [3] *Ibid.*, x., 39.

everything within His form—the Gods, men, and all, within one divine image of intolerable glory. Arjuna is startled, is terrified, is shaken, is confused, is crushed. He cries out finally in his human longing: "This Thy forth-streaming life bewilders me. . . . Again I fain would see Thee as before; put on again Thy four-armed shape, O Lord."[1] Arjuna's experience is a universal one. While we grow, God must narrow Himself to our limited knowledge, otherwise we shall never learn to know Him at all. You cannot pour into a vessel more than the vessel can contain; the liquid only overflows on every side; and the great Ocean of Brahman cannot flow in its entirety into these tiny vessels that we present for its reception; only as the vessel expands can more and more of that illimitable Self pour itself thereinto.

So then we have in Hinduism rites, ceremonies, observances, images, countless forms of worship adapted to the countless types of human knowledge and of human ignorance. But they are all adapted to draw out love; they are all adapted to stimulate devotion; they are all adapted to bring about worship; because it is this attitude of the soul that is important, and not the intellectual form in which the worship is couched. By these means men gradually rise to the one supreme image of Him who is the Lord of the Universe; they rise to the conception of Íshvara, the one Lord above all. And by this means are they prevented from dragging down

[1] *Bhagavad Gîtâ*, xi., 31, 46.

the sublime conception of the one God to the low levels of their early ignorance, making the Lord of the universe the image of human passions, moving within human limitations. They are constantly reminded that they do not know God as He is, but only a little ray of Him, as much as they have capacity to receive. And as they grow, they realize with delight that more of Him flows into the conception of Him that they adore, expanding it, illuminating it, subliming it, till it seems to yield some vision of His glory. Rising to Íshvara they may worship Him as Vishnu or in any of Vishnu's Avatâras. They may worship Him as Shiva, the great Yogî, the Lord of Wisdom. Then they have reached the conception of the One which underlies the many in manifestation.

Now we must see—for we have to hurry on—how all this was worked out in the individual life of the soul, looked at externally in the stages of its evolution through the three worlds; by the individual life I mean the whole life of the soul from the time it began its experience as a human soul, *i.e.*, from the formation of the Kârana Sharîra,[1] to the time when it reaches Brahman and is a perfect reflection of the divine. Hinduism divides that individual life into four great stages, represented by the fourfold order of castes. You have there the evolution, stage after stage, of the individual soul. In Hinduism, as the model polity for the Áryan race, it was made part of the social fabric of the nation, but wherever the

[1] The causal body, lasting through the human cycle.

soul may be evolved it has to pass through the four stages, in inner realities though not in outer births. Hinduism was made to represent the inner growth in outer form, that men might learn spiritual truths by seeing the external pictures. Let us glance at them in succession, seeing what the soul was meant to learn in each, and how the environment was adapted to the advancing evolution. The lowest stage was that of the Shûdra, where there was little obligation save the duty of obedience and service. The next stage was that of the Vaishya, where wealth was permitted, its gathering was encouraged, and the soul had to learn unselfishness in the possession of wealth; the rightful use of wealth in service is the lesson of the caste. Then the third stage was trodden, that of the Kshatriya, where life itself was to be held as sacrifice, and not only material goods. And finally comes the caste of the Brâhmanas, wherein nothing that is transitory should have power to attract, and wherein the soul is dwelling in its last body upon earth. And beyond the four castes, when these have been lived through and their lessons learned, stands the Sannyâsi, who has no caste, nor uses rites nor ceremonies, nor fires, nor possesses anything that belongs to the passing existence—the Sannyâsi of the heart, not only of the cloth. So thoroughly is he apart from personality that men in greeting him say only, "Namo Nârâyanâya," praising the God in him instead of greeting the outer form.

This caste system makes the political fabric of the

nation; the spiritual teaching, under the exoteric expression, gave rise to this fourfold order.

Next, we must glance at the personal life, *i.e.*, the life that is led in the three worlds through one personal life-cycle, one period in each world. There again the life varies according to the stage reached by the individual, that is, by his stage in the whole life of the soul. In the early stage he will have the simple life of the senses with a little of the lower mind, and will spend considerable time in Bhuvarloka and a brief time in Svargaloka. As he advances intellectually, the stay in Bhuvarloka will shorten, and that in Svargaloka will lengthen, his desires being of a nature to find fruition chiefly in the higher world. Let us take a case of yet higher order to show the earthly life in its highest stage before actual Yoga is practised, lived so as to minimize life in Bhuvarloka and to extend the bliss of Svargaloka.

The personal life on earth is divided into four stages, or âshramas. First, the life of the student, where he has as it were to rehearse in the new body all the virtues he had to learn in his past evolution when he belonged to the Shûdra caste—obedience, discipline, reverence, chastity, industry, duty to those above him, these are the expressions of the life required from the Hindu student—the first stage of this personal life. Then comes the second stage, the stage of the married home, of the man as citizen, as husband, as father of a family, discharging his duties alike to the State and to the home. This is the second or grihastha stage, the school of unselfish virtue, penetrated through and through with religion. He must perform the five daily sacrifices, the sacrifices to the Gods, to the Pitris, to the Rishis, to men, and to animals—teaching the round of daily duty of unselfish charity. Thus were all debts paid to the invisible and the visible, and the daily obligations of every kind discharged. There were further special ceremonies, marking every family event, ceremonies connected with the ante-natal life of a child, ceremonies at birth, ceremonies at marriage, ceremonies at death, ceremonies after death, following the soul onwards into the invisible world—all these laid down as the spiritual fabric within which the soul was to develop. The noblest ideal of married life ever given to the world is found in Hinduism, of husband and wife drawn together by spiritual affinity rather than by fleshly desire, and joined in the bonds of an indissoluble marriage, joined for spiritual development, for spiritual growth; the man unable to perform many of the religious ceremonies without the wife, the wife being the shishya, the pupil, of the husband, who was guru as well as spouse. See the life led within the family, the beautiful relationship of sons to father, of sons to mother, of brothers to sisters, and so on; all laid down with care and discrimination, always with the eye fixed on the one idea—to develop the dawning quality of spiritual love in man. Then the insistence on moral virtues, the constant holding up in the great literature, familiar in every household, of the very noblest ideals, ideals in which men lived the common life of men and were yet patterns of noblest virtue, expressing the very loftiest purity and righteousness of life. Is there any literature that gives to the training of the young heart nobler examples to follow in every department of human life? Could your daughters have better examples, say, of wifely love, than in Sîtâ and Savitrî? Could they have nobler inspiration to win knowledge than the examples of Gargî and Maitreyî? Where will you find grander types of humanity, perfect in all the different circumstances of life? If you take patterns of virtue, can you find a nobler trio anywhere than the three brothers, Râma, Lakshmana, and Bharata? Can you find brotherly devotion, brotherly love, brotherly service anywhere more exquisitely delineated? Can you find more fervent love between husband and wife than that between Râma and Sîtâ? Can you find nobler example of exquisite balance of mind, of patience, of serenity than in the exiled ruler Yudhishthira? Can you find anywhere duty more perfectly incarnated than in Bhîshma, lying on his bed of arrows and pouring out divinest wisdom to the younger lives who gathered round him? Thus was the soul trained by precept and example, thus stage by stage was the soul led on in daily practice. Then follow the last two stages of life, when the family duties were fulfilled—life in the forest, husband and wife carrying out with them the household fire which had been lighted at the time of their marriage, and leading there a life of peaceful contemplation away from the world, leaving full-grown sons behind them to carry on the duties of the state and the home; and then the final stage of the recluse, of the ascetic, where the soul was left face to face with Brahman. Such was the life, orderly and progressive, self-restrained and dignified, by which the soul was trained and developed until the time came when there were open before it the three paths, or Mârgas, the practice of Yoga commencing in the two later stages of the preceding lives.

We have arrived at the third division of our subject—the science of Yoga, the way by which a man may hasten his evolution, expand his consciousness, and rise into union with the Supreme. Yoga was the final stage of an evolution patiently trodden with ever-increasing recognition of the goal, from the worship of the lower Devatas[1] through the four castes, through the four âshramas, up to the direct training for the liberation of the soul from the wheel of births and deaths.

As just said, three are the paths, and each has its own Yoga: Karma Mârga, the final stage of which is Karma Yoga; Gnyâna Mârga, ending with Gnyâna Yoga; Bhakti Mârga, ending in Bhakti Yoga.[2] For all the subdual of the senses and the control of the mind are essential prerequi-

[1] Lower Gods, including the astral entities who are busied with the processes of nature on the two lowest planes.

[2] The path of action; the path of wisdom; the path of devotion. Yoga, or union with the Self, may be practised and attained by any one of these three ways.

sites, but the methods to accomplish this differ with the paths.

In the Karma Mârga a man learns by constant practice in daily life; in the home he practises restraint of the senses, is self-denying, self-sacrificing; he gains control of the mind by his daily meditation, by accuracy and diligence in his business, by utilizing the constant opportunities of maintaining concentration and balance amid the distractions and in the whirl of the common life of men. When by lives of such effort he has prepared himself, he begins the Karma Yoga, by which he learns to perform action as duty, without desire for fruit, "renouncing the fruits of action," as it is called. He performs every duty with scrupulous fidelity, but he looks for no fruit from it, he renounces all results. Finally he performs every action as sacrifice to the Supreme, his only motive the doing of the will of Íshvara. By this, though living in the world, he has no attachments and is at heart the unattached, the wanderer. By this, he builds his "hut" and has his solitary place for meditation. By this he realizes the pure "I" and its unity with other "I's," and is the Hamsa. By this he rises above the "I" and becomes the Paramahamsa.[1] By renunciation and sacrifice Ahamkâra[2] is destroyed, and with its destruction the blinding veils fall away from his eyes, and he is filled with Gnyâna and Bhakti, for the end of the three paths is one.

[1] These stages are described below in the Gnyâna Mârga.

[2] The quality of I-ness, separateness.

For the Gnyâna Mârga a man develops his intellect by study pursued through many lives, till he has reached a point at which he begins to weary of mere knowledge, and seeks the permanent truth, of which all knowledges are the broken gleams. Then he must develop Viveka, discrimination between the real and the unreal; Vairâgya, disgust for the unreal; Shatsampatti, the six mental qualifications—Shama, control of the mind; Dama, control of the body; Uparati, wide-minded tolerance; Titiksha, endurance; Shraddhâ, faith; Samadhâna, balance; he must have Mumuksha, the longing for liberation from the transitory; and then, with all these, he is the Adhikari, the man fitted to receive initiation into Yoga.[1] Then he follows the Gnyâna Yoga, and, discerning the valuelessness of the transitory, he becomes the Parivrajaka, the wanderer, unattached by desire, the homeless man. By yet deeper vision he realizes the permanent and rests on that as his secure foundation, so becoming the Kutîchaka, the dweller in the hut, abiding in that one secure resting-place. Then he feels the self-consciousness clearly, realizes the "I," and sees the same "I" in others, the Hamsa stage. Rising above it, as the spiritual vision is clarified and consciousness expands, he becomes the Paramahamsa, beyond the "I," and realizes "I am He."

Bhakti Mârga is trodden by the soul whose affec-

[1] These were the qualifications demanded by Shrî Shankarâchârya ere a man was allowed to study his Vedânta, for the Vedânta cannot be realized without Yoga.

tions are drawn towards some manifested aspect of God, and its early stages are those of devoted worship, of deep love and reverence. Gradually the soul takes on the qualities it worships, becoming that which it adores. The non-attachment gained by renunciation in Karma Mârga, by discrimination in Gnyâna Mârga, it gains by expelling all lower attachments by the one attachment to its Lord; by love it conquers all baser desires, and they wither for lack of expression. Sacrifice is a joyful acting out of devotion; each of the four stages is trodden, with love, in each case, as the active means of accomplishment, until the love that worshipped finds the object of its worship embracing it, and feels itself merging into complete unity with its Beloved.

In truth the three paths blend, and in the higher stages you cannot separate the one from the other; for the Karma Yogi is full of Bhakti, and also by his sacrifice destroys Ahamkâra and thus becomes perfect in wisdom. The Gnyâni and the Bhakta each take on the qualities of the other. In the heart of the Bhakta wisdom arises spontaneously, and in the heart of the Gnyâni Bhakti flowers as the inevitable result of vision.

In the later stages of each path, so soon as His services are needed, the Guru appears and takes the soul under His own guidance; the man becomes a shishya, a chelâ.[1] He comes not to the unprepared, the unready, though the impatience of man often cries out for His presence when that presence would

[1] A disciple, or pupil.

be unheeded were it there. He leads the soul through the later stages, giving such adjusting aid as is required, helping it to unfold its own capacities, the divine potentialities within it, thus hastening its evolution until achievement is reached. Then the chelâ, in his turn, becomes the liberated soul, ready and fit to help onwards the less advanced. He becomes the Jîvanmukta,[1] living in the body still, to be a link between humanity physical and humanity spiritual, a channel of divine love and strength to man. Or he may become the Videhamukta,[2] living in the invisible world, still yielding service to the One, still carrying out the divine purpose, serving in other ways as channel of spiritual life to men. These mighty Ones pay Their debts to Their own Gurus by service of the present and of the future humanities, acting as Gurus to present and future shishyas, just as They received Their own illumination from Gurus developed in the past. Thus universe succeeds universe, each aiding its successes, until our thought fails to express itself, and the human faculty sinks down unable to soar farther.

Such briefly, most imperfectly expressed, such is the religion founded in immemorial antiquity, that has come down from the Rishis. Such ought to be your religion, heirs of the past, descendants of those mighty ones! Just in so far as you live it, in so far are you really their heirs. Just in so far as this is dear to you and practised by you, are you learning

[1] The liberated soul.

[2] The liberated bodiless one.

the lesson of evolution as it was taught by Them, and given to the people They instructed; just so far are you profiting by opportunities greater than those offered to any other nation, opportunities that, wasted, will be bewailed by you under less favorable conditions in many a life to come.

ZOROASTRIANISM.

My Brothers, one of the differences which are continually arising between occult knowledge and the Oriental science which has of late years been growing up in the West, is the question of the age of the great religions. When we come to Buddhism and to Christianity the difference is limited to the question of a century or two. But with regard both to Hinduism and Zoroastrianism there is an entire conflict between Orientalism and Occultism—a clash which does not seem likely to cease: for most certainly the Occultists will not change their position, and the Orientalists, on the other hand, are likely only to be driven backwards stage by stage with the unveiling of ancient cities, with the discovery of ancient monuments. And this is a slow process. Hinduism and Zoroastrianism go back into what history would call "the night of time," Hinduism being the more ancient, and Zoroastrianism the second religion in the evolution of the Áryan race.

I propose to look at the changes of opinion through which Orientalists have passed, in order to show you how they are gradually being forced backwards, disputing, we may say, every inch of the ground, century after century, as the growing evidence points to an ever greater antiquity. Then I will take up the occult testimony, and see where that places the religion of the Iranian Prophet

Some writers, we find, on glancing over their works, place this prophet—called Zoroaster sometimes, and more lately Zarathushtra (and I must ask the pardon of my Parsî brethren, as I may be committing the most flagrant mispronunciations, for I am absolutely ignorant of the Avestaic language)—as late as 610 B.C. That would make him about contemporary with the Buddha and with Plato—a position resting on Mahometan authority, and if ever seriously entertained by European Orientalists now at least entirely renounced. Dr. L. H. Mills—looked upon as one of the greatest European authorities, who made the standard translation of the Gâthâs and published with it the various other authoritative translations—in dealing with this question of antiquity, relies on the evidence of language, a point on which I shall have something to say a little later. He says that the Gâthâs are written in a tongue which is evidently related to the Vaidic Sanskrit, the Gâthâs being "long after the oldest Riks."[1] Now the *Rig Veda* is put by him at the preposterously late date of only 4,000 years before Christ; and basing himself on that date he puts the Gâthâs at 1000 B.C., and possibly as far back as 1500 B.C. So that we have got from 610 B.C. to 1000 B.C. or even 1500 B.C. as our first backward step. But Dr. Mills says that they may be much older—as, in truth,

[1] *Zendavesta*, Introduction, p. 37. Sacred Books of the East, xxxi.

they are. In his later work, writing in 1890, he says: "I have ceased to resist the conviction that the latter limit [B.C. 1500] may be put farther back. If they antedate the worship of Mithra . . . there is no telling how old they may be. The decision of criticism is to refrain from conjectures too closely limiting their age."[1]

Then we come to the view taken by the German savant, Dr. Haug, and we find that he contends for a greater antiquity, basing himself on the destruction of the library of Persepolis by Alexander, in 329 B.C. He argues that, in order that such a vast library, such a mass of literature, should have been gathered together, you must assume a greater antiquity, to give the mere time necessary for the writing and the gathering of the books. The writing was completed, he thinks, about 400 B.C. It is not possible, he says, at the very latest, to put the time of Zoroaster after 1000 B.C., and the regards 2800 B.C. as a more likely date, while he may be very much older.[2] Dr. Haug further remarks: "Under no circumstances can we assign him a later date than B.C. 1000, and one may even find reasons for placing his era much earlier and making him a contemporary of Moses. Pliny, who compares both Moses and Zoroaster,

[1] *A Study of five Zaruthushtrian* (*Zoroastrian*) *Gâthâs*, with Pahlavi translation, Naryosangh's Sanskrit Text and the Persian text translated, and a commentary. Introduction, pp. xix., xx.

[2] *Essays on the Parsîs*, by Martin Haug, Ph.D., Trübner's Oriental Series, p. 136.

whom he calls inventors of two different kinds of magic rites, goes much further and states that Zoroaster lived several thousand years before Moses."[1]

So we are gradually getting backward, from 610 B.C. to 1500 B.C.; from 1500 B.C. to 2800 B.C., and possibly very much earlier, may be the first proclamation of the famous truths by the Prophet. Greek testimony, however, which is available—and it is valuable as being much more ancient than the views of our modern Orientalists—throws the date, once more, very much farther back. Aristotle, for instance, places the date of the Prophet at 9600 B.C., putting it 6,000 years before the time of Plato, and we may say generally that this is the view which is taken by the Greek historians. Somewhere about 9,000 years before the Christian era would be the date assigned by them to the teachings of the Prophet.[2] The discoveries now being made by European archæologists are very much helping the contention which pushes the beginnings of the religion farther and farther back; for, inasmuch as we have to connect this Zarathushtrian tradition with the tradition of Chaldea, with the tradition of Nineveh, and of Babylonia, the late researches in those districts throw some light upon the question. You may remember that only a month or two ago in *Lucifer*, in a comment on an article by H. P. Blavatsky, I mentioned some of the very latest discoveries which are being made in the country over which this religion once ruled unchallenged. We find there the

[1] *Ibid.* p. 299. [2] *Ibid.* p. 298.

history of that land, preserved in cuneiform writing, traced back to at least seven thousand years before Christ, and probably, the discoverer says, to 8000 B.C. This cuneiform writing is now under process of translation, and it is possible that, when that translation is published, evidence which even European science will accept may be available corroborative of the antiquity of the religion of Zoroaster.

Occultism, in any case, throws the beginnings of his teachings far, far back, age after age behind all these dates. Occultists have two kinds of records on which they rely. First, the great Brotherhood has preserved the ancient writings—the writings themselves, taken away at the time when they were written; these writings are stored in underground temples, underground libraries, where no enemy can find them and where no injury can touch them. There, millennium after millennium, the knowledge of the world is gathered in its written form, and there are people to-day, men and women to-day, who have been permitted to set eyes on many of these ancient writings—writings the very knowledge of which has passed from the world of profane history, writings in the ancient sacerdotal language, different from anything which the most ancient of the races now knows. That is not the only record on which the occultist depends; he depends also on those imperishable records written, as we sometimes say, in the Akâsha itself; meaning by that that there is a subtle medium which, to use a physical analogy, records like a sensitive plate every event that happens, even in its minutest details—the photograph, as it were, of the evolution of man, correct down to the very tiniest incident, and which at any time may be referred to, at any moment may be read, by those who train themselves for the study, who are willing to undergo the discipline necessary for such a research. Thus the record can be verified by each successive inquirer; we have the testimony of expert after expert who studies these most ancient records, and who sees not mere written characters but the events of the past, moving in living accuracy before him, moving as they occurred, instinct with life. The events of the history behind us thus live in the past of time.

According to those records, this religion which in modern days is called Zoroastrianism, the religion of the Parsîs, is, as I said, the second of the religions of the Áryan stock. The Iranians, coming forth from the same cradle-land as the first family, but spreading westwards over that vast extent of territory which includes not only modern Persia but the realm of ancient Persia, were led in their first migration thither by their great Prophet Zoroaster, who held to them the same position that Manu held to the whole original Áryan race. He belonged to the same mighty Brotherhood, and was a high Initiate of the same great Lodge, taught by the same Teachers, the Sons of the Fire. Many of you will have read in those most ancient records from the Book of Dzyân, given in the *Secret Doctrine*[1] of the Sons of

[1] *Op. cit.*, by H. P. Blavatsky, i., stanza iv., 1.

the Fire, who were the Instructors of all the great Initiates, called in Their turn the Lords of the Flame. He came as a teacher at the beginning of this Iranian subrace, to give them the ancient truths in a form fitted for a civilization that was to grow up amongst them; in a form fitted for the type of mind which was to develop amongst them, suited to train, to evolve, to develop them, just as other faiths were given to other peoples with the same object and on similar lines. From that mighty Teacher—whose date runs backward to a time at which every Orientalist would laugh in scorn—from Him came down a line of prophets that superintended the earlier development of the Iranian people. And here let me remind you that, when we are speaking of such a line of prophets, it by no means follows that each prophet is a separate individual, for the same soul often reincarnates time after time in the same office, as you know well enough from your own ancient records. Such men as, say, Veda Vyâsa, had not one birth only upon earth but many births, for those men are always living in touch with earth, They are always superintending the spiritual evolution of mankind, and They come forth from time to time, from age to age, manifesting in a body of the time at which They appear, the same great Teacher, the same liberated Soul, the same mighty Instructor, over and over again taking the same name, as though to suggest the spiritual identity to the deaf ears of men. And tracing down this line of prophets, or this Prophet, we begin to see where the Greek tradition comes in, and we understand that the Zoroaster spoken of by Aristotle ninety-six hundred years before what we call the time of Christ (dated of course by him from Plato, not from Christ) was seventh of this name from the original Zoroaster, and not the first Zoroaster as the Greeks supposed, and as I imagine too often many of the modern Parsîs are willing to believe. He then was seventh in the line of teachers who came to revive and reinforce the teaching when it was sinking downward, and was menaced with overthrow. Still later than that there was another Zoroaster, about the year 4000 before Christ, who again revived the ancient teaching, again repeated the essential truths, giving them forth again with divine authority, and by means of that sacred fire which is the symbol of Deity and which is in truth the voice of Deity. As we study this succession of prophets we see that from this ancient religion came what is called the "great science," the "Magic" of the Chaldees. We understand that the Magi of antiquity were teachers and priests of this same ancient faith, and—if, for a moment, I may startle the modern mind—that when more than 20,000 years ago the Chaldean sage stood on the roof of his observatory and marked and recorded the passage of the stars, that man was one of the comparatively modern descendants of the long line of the Magi, one of the comparatively modern representatives of the ancient lore of the Zoroastrian faith.

Let us then go backward and look at the teaching

in the light of its earlier form, even although we have only its later recensions so far as scholarship is concerned; and we shall find that even in its later recensions the ancient truths are recognizable though hidden; and that though many of these truths have been distorted in the modern form, have been materialized, have been degraded, still the occultist may recognize them; still he may point them out to those who follow this ancient religion, and may pray the modern Parsîs, in the name of their ancient Prophet, the divine Initiate who founded their faith, to rise above the modern materialism, to rise above the too petty limits of modern Orientalism, and to claim their rightful dignity as one of the most ancient of the world's religions. Let them link themselves to the immemorial occult tradition, and not degrade themselves by accepting every passing suggestion of European scholarship.

Let it be remembered, as we shall find proved by language presently, that these ancient Iranians were Áryan and not Semitic. That is one of the points on which dispute has arisen, and in a moment I will show you how the language bears out the occult contention. We admit, of course, in much later days a Semitic intermixture. But the Iranians came from the Áryan stock, and are really a sister race of the Áryans south of the Himâlayas.

The first Zoroaster, in teaching again the essential principles which are the foundation of every faith, and in each faith are apt to be overlaid by later accretions, blended philosophy and religion in a remarkable way. Coming to found a civilization which had its own peculiar features, which was essentially agricultural in its character, which was permeated through and through with the idea of the practical side of life, which was intended to train men practically in a noble faith and sublime morality, He did not give a metaphysical philosophy and an exoteric religion, linking the two together; but He interblended the two so that it is well-nigh impossible to give an account of each separately. A better idea of the whole is obtained by following His method, and by studying the philosophy and the religion as a single system. Having foresight of the special civilization that was to grow up, He gave an immense amount of astronomical science interwoven with the philosophy and the religious teaching, and He gave that astronomical science—so necessary for people engaged in agriculture—in its occult form, and not in its poor dwarfed modern presentation. To Him the stars were not mere masses of matter, revolving by blind unconscious laws around dead unconscious suns. To Him the planets around the sun, and the mighty stars in the highest heavens, were but the bodies of spiritual Intelligences, whose will was their guiding law and whose knowledge insured the stability of the universe. He taught astronomy not as of dead matter and soulless energy, but as of living Intelligences, moving in changeless order, because guided by perfect wisdom and unswerving will. He taught astronomy as the living occult science of spiritual wisdom, expressed in the material universe, the lowest form of its expression. Out of the teaching of religious philosophy and of science there grew up the ethic which down to the present day is the glory of the Zoroastrian creed. A perfect practical purity is the keynote of that morality, purity in every action of the personal life, purity in every relation to external nature, honoring external elements as the manifestations of the divine purity, guarding, as it were, their spotless cleanliness as a homage to the Life wherefrom the whole proceeds. We shall find as we go on that these are the salient points of His teachings, but ere I take them up one by one I must glance at this question of the language, for we need to understand that question to some extent if we are to trace the teachings through the different books that at present are in our hands.

I have said that the language in its oldest form, the language of the *Avesta*, justifies the occult statement of the antiquity of the Zoroastrian faith; for by the testimony—and I am quite willing to take it when it supports the occult view—by the testimony of European Orientalists this Avestaic language, even as it is to-day in the latest recensions, is an Âryan dialect and is allied to the Sanskrit of the Vedas. There is no time, and it would be a little outside the subject, to say anything of the changes which you will know occurred in the development of Sanskrit in this country, the changes which are noticeable between the Sanskrit of the Vedas and the classical Sanskrit of later days; but the *Avesta* is allied to the early, to the Vaidik Sanskrit,[1] and that Sanskrit, as our German doctor tells us, is an elder sister of the Avestaic language.[2] Not only is this similarity clearly and distinctly marked in the words that are used, but the similarity goes far beyond the words themselves. These ancient Gâthâs, or hymns, are written in metres that are closely allied to the metres of the *Sama Veda*. Their rhythm, their feet, the evident method of their chanting, is a very close ally of the rhythm, of the feet, of the chanting, which still exist amongst the Hindus. So that we find, looking at them, that this mark of antiquity is upon them, and as we throw back, despite the Orientalists, the antiquity of the Vedas, the antiquity of Hinduism, we carry back also with us the antiquity of the Zoroastrian faith, linking the two together in our defence as they were linked together in their earlier days in the far past of the two great peoples. So again, if I may for a moment take the occult record, the chants are the same. Those wonderful chants of the ancient world, which have their results in the invisible, those chants that control the lower intelligences and that rise up to the higher in the language of color and of music—these Gâthâs were chanted in that same archaic svara, and, though lost by the priests of modern Zoroastrianism, the echoes are still recoverable from the Ákâshic records. Turning now—for the survey is necessarily hasty—from the language of the *Avesta* to that much contested word "Zend," which some say is a language

[1] *Essays on the Parsîs*, p. 70. [2] *Ibid.*, p. 40.

while others say it is a commentary—how far does European scholarship throw light upon the question? They say, some scholars—and here I fear modern Parsîs tend to agree with them—that Zend is nothing more than a modern Pahlavi translation and commentary on the ancient writings. The word is constantly applied simply to that translation, made certainly under the Sasanian dynasty in comparatively modern times. But I am glad to see that some European scholarship rejects that contention, and declares that the Zend is the original commentary written in the language of the *Avesta*, and is therefore thrown back again to the ancient times, to the times of the language allied to the Sanskrit of the Vedas. Dr. Haug says that from the "use of the denomination Avesta and Zend by the Pahlavi translators we are fully entitled to conclude that the Zend they mentioned was the commentary on the Avesta already existing before they undertook their translation; and as they considered it sacred, this Zend was probably in the same language as the original Avesta. . . . Originally it (Zend) meant the commentaries made by the successors of Zarathushtra upon the sacred writings of the prophet and his immediate disciples. These commentaries must have been written in nearly the same language as the original text, and, as that language gradually became unintelligible to all but the priests, the commentaries were regarded as part of the text, and a new explanation, or Zend, was required. This new Zend was furnished by the most learned priests of the Sasanian period, in the shape of a translation into Pahlavi, the vernacular language of Persia in those days; and in later times the term Zend has been confined to this translation."[1] The contention that Zend was a commentary is to a large extent shown to be true, if once more we turn to the occult testimony instead of to the testimony of modern scholarship. For we find, and here we may take the evidence of H. P. Blavatsky—who was writing of that which was within her own knowledge from her own study under her Teacher, under her Guru—that this commentary, the original Zend of the Iranians, was a commentary written in a language derived from that ancient sacerdotal language to which I alluded in the beginning of this lecture. For there is a language known to all occultists, not a language of letters, as letters are understood in our modern tongues, a language of signs, of symbols, of colors, of sounds, which rings out in music as well as shines in color, and which takes its own forms, which every Initiate can recognize and translate into the lower languages of the intellectual world. It has sometimes been called the Zenzar. It has sometimes been called the Deva-Bhâshya. H. P. Blavatsky says of Zend: "It means, as in one sense correctly stated, 'a commentary or explanation'; but it also means that which the Orientalists do not seem to have any idea about, *viz.*, the 'rendering of the esoteric sentences,' the veil used to conceal the correct meaning of the Zen-d-zar texts, the sacerdotal language in use among the Initiates

[1] *Essays on the Parsis*, pp. 120, 122.

of archaic India. Found now in several undecipherable inscriptions, it is still used and studied to this day in the secret communities of the Eastern adepts, and called by them—according to the locality—*Zend-zar* and *Brahma* or *Deva Bhâshya*. . . . The Zend text is simply a secret *code* of certain words and expressions agreed upon by the original compilers, and the key to which is but with the Initiates."[1] Many names have been given to the language; names matter not, for they vary with every tongue; but the essential thing is that such a language exists, that it is known to-day as it was known a million years ago, that people learn it now as they learned it then, that occult instruction is given in that language, and not in the clumsy sounds articulated by a physical tongue, and that from that language truths are translated into the most ancient intellectual tongues derived from it. The Vaidik Sanskrit is the most ancient intellectual echo of that archaic language, and the Zend of the Iranian has the same root, comes from the same fount. Later on, when we come to the Pahlavi translations, we find there that we are within what is generally called historic time. "Pahlavi" is now applied only to "the written language of Persia during the Sasanian dynasty, and to the literature of that period and a short time after,"[2] but in earlier times it was used generally

[1] *Theosophist*, IV., article on Zoroastrianism, commencing on p. 224.

[2] *Essays on the Parsis*, p. 81. The Sasanian dynasty flourished from A.D. 226 to A.D. 653, when it was swept away by the Mahommedans.

for ancient Persian. Here we have Semitic words, traces of the Semitic influence, and it is contended that these run backwards to some six hundred years before the time of Christ.[1] That matters not, for six hundred years before the time of Christ is a modern time for an occultist. He is dealing with millennia and not with centuries, and this sign of Semitic influence in the later time has absolutely no influence on his judgment as to the origin of the ancient faith. We must pass from this question of language, which might well be worked out at greater length and which leads to many other matters of interest, to one other disputed point of importance, too much overlooked. The Chaldean tradition, as it is preserved through the Grecian nation, is of vital interest, although it be at present ignored, as, I understand, by the modern Zoroastrianism. This Chaldean tradition which comes through Greece may roughly be said to have arisen as follows. In the time of Alexander it is admitted that there was a vast library at Persepolis, but, as you know, he burned it either in drunkenness or in revenge. Hence he is constantly called "the accursed Alexander" in all the later writings belonging to the faith of Zoroaster. Now there is evidence that at the time of that burning there were two complete sets of the whole Zoroastrian literature. One of these sets was in the library and was burnt by this "accursed Alexander." The other set was taken possession of by the Greek conquerors, and by them was translated into Greek. Little of this survives,

[1] *Ibid.*, p. 81.

but fragments of it remain in the *Nabathæan Agriculture*, in the quotations made from it by Neo-Platonic writers, who speak of the *Oracles of Zoroaster* and of the teachings of that Prophet. These traces of the ancient teaching, preserved in the literature of the Greeks, strengthen and corroborate the acknowledged Zoroastrian tradition. Why then should not this assistance be accepted in the struggle to substantiate the antiquity of the religion? Why should not modern Parsîs take the evidence which comes down to them through this other line, since the two lines are found to blend into one? These fragments preserved by Greek authors, borne witness to in the literature of the Greek nation, these fragments still breathe the ancient spirit, and corroborate the teachings which Zoroaster in the past has given.

Let us now turn to the literature itself, and consider our documents. First comes the *Yasna*, of which the most ancient part consists of the Gâthâs, the archaic hymns, the teachings which came from the mouth of the great Prophet Himself. They are now only five in number, and, as accepted in the present day, are mere fragments, but they are dignified, sublime, and grand, bearing testimony to the nobility of the ancient teaching. These form the first part of the *Yasna;* the second part consists of prayers and ceremonies—prayers addressed to the supreme Deity, prayers equally addressed to the mighty ones who stand below Him, forming the spiritual hierarchy. For ancient Zoroastrianism knew nothing of that modern materialism which tries to place God at one pole of the universe and man and his world at the other, with a mighty gap of bare and empty space between them. In Zoroastrianism, as in every other ancient faith, there was no gap in the universe, no empty space, no place where there were not living Intelligences, no place where spiritual beings were not working; from man near the base of the ladder to the supreme God at its head, there were ranged Intelligences growing higher and higher, diviner and diviner, and all these were objects of adoration—a fact to which the whole literature of Zoroastrianism bears testimony. After the *Yasna*, with its two parts, we have the *Visparad*, a collection of invocations, of preparatory invocations to be used before other prayers and sacrifices. These two, the *Yasna* and the *Visparad*, may be regarded as holding the position in Zoroastrianism that is held by the Vedas in Hinduism. Below these there comes what was once a vast mass of literature, of which only, alas! the names for the most part survive. There is one book complete, and some few fragments of the remainder, out of a list of twenty-one great treatises, of which the contents, roughly outlined, are also on record—the twenty-one Nasks they are called. These deal with sciences of every kind, with medicine, with astronomy, with agriculture, with botany, with philosophy, with the whole range in fact of sciences and laws; they hold the position held by the Vedânga in Hinduism. I lay stress on these analogies, because they so much strengthen our position as to the antiquity and the dignity of this ancient faith. Of these only one book survives in its entirety, the *Vendidad*, the book of laws affecting the preservation of purity alike in external nature and in man. Next we have the *Khordah Avesta* or little *Avesta*, consisting of Yashts (invocations) and of prayers, for the use of the laity rather than of the priests, many of them the prayers used daily by the modern Parsîs. It is a mixed collection—some of the fragments very ancient, some of comparatively recent date. After the burning of the library of Persepolis came a period of five hundred and fifty years of anarchy and tumult, and it was only at the close of this period that, under the Sasanian monarchs, the surviving fragments of Zoroastrian literature were gathered together. Little marvel that but fragments remained, fragments of a once glorious whole, like pieces of mosaic rent from their bed where they formed part of a great and intelligible picture. Only those who can recover the picture can see where each fragment fitted in, and can thus judge of the original beauty of the whole.

I have explained rather at length—considering the time at my disposal—though very briefly in reality, these preliminary details, because to most people they are almost unknown, and yet, unless they are known, it is impossible to appreciate the weight of evidence by which the antiquity of the philosophy and the religion themselves are sustained. And we may also say that it is necessary to see where the gaps in the evidence occur, to appreciate how much has been lost, how fragmentary are the Scriptures remaining in our hands, and how imperfect must therefore be any statement of the philosophy and the religion drawn from them alone. Enough, however, remains to substantiate the proposition that Zoroastrianism is at one with occult teaching on all important points, save one. In the Scriptures, as accepted by orthodox Parsîs, reincarnation is not found; it is taught in the fragments preserved by the Greeks, and in the *Desatir*, a book containing much occult truth, but none of these are regarded as authoritative.

Let us now turn to the philosophy and the religion themselves, and as there has been, most unfortunately, a materialistic reaction, under European influence, it is necessary to quote verse by verse from the received Scriptures in order to establish the ancient occult teachings.

At the head of the manifested universe stands Ahura-Mazdâo, sometimes translated as the living Wisdom, sometimes as the Lord of Wisdom, sometimes as the Wise Lord. The cuneiform inscriptions have Aûramazdâ, the Sasanian Aûharmazda, and the modern Persian is Hôrmazd or Ormazd.[1]

He is the Supreme, He is the Universal, the All-pervasive, the Source and the Fountain of Life; He, in the Zoroastrian religion, holds the same position as the manifested Brahman of the Upanishads, who

[1] *Essays on the Parsîs*, p. 302.

came forth at the beginning, the One, the source of life to man. He is described over and over again in the different Scriptures, not so fully in the Gâthâs—though there also in part—as in some of the prayers and invocations. Let us take two specimens to show what is the description given of this mighty Being, in order that you may realize how sublime is the conception, how lofty this idea of the primeval God. In the *Ormazd Yasht*, He proclaims His own qualities, something in the same way as Shrî Krishna does in the Tenth Discourse in the *Bhagavad Gîtâ*. He proclaims His names, the names which describe His attributes. He says: "I am the Protector, I am the Creator, I am the Nourisher, I am the Knowing, I am the Holiest Heavenly One. My name is the Healing . . . My name is God, my name is Great, Wise One; My name is the Pure . . . I am called the Majestic . . . the Far-seeing . . . I am called the Watcher . . . The Augmenter," and so on through a list of seventy-two names.[1] Let us listen to the description of Him in the words of the great Prophet Himself: "He (Ahura-Mazda) first created, through His inborn lustre, the multitude of celestial bodies, and through His intellect the good creatures, governed by the inborn good mind. Thou, Ahura-Mazda, the Spirit who art everlasting, makest them (the good creatures) grow. When my eyes behold Thee, the Essence of Truth, the Creator of life, who manifests His life in His works, then I know Thee to be the primeval Spirit, Thou, Mazda, so high in

[1] *Ormazd Yasht*, trans. from Prof. Spiegel by A. H. Bleek.

mind as to create the world, and the father of the good mind."[1] Ahura-Mazdâo is revealed as threefold, and we read in the *Khorda Avesta*: "Praise to Thee, Ahura-Mazda, threefold before other creatures."[2] Notice this "threefold," for it is of vital importance. It joins this Zoroastrian conception of the First Being to the threefold or triple Brahman who is so familiar to us in the Upanishads, and it also explains His emanating two principles which exist in Him, and a third completing the Trinity, two principles which too often have been placed as opposing principles, making the Zoroastrian teaching essentially dualistic instead of essentially monistic, as it is. But before taking up that point we must recognize that according to the ancient teaching there was behind and beyond Ahura-Mazdâo the One, the Unknowable, that "Boundless Time" who by Orientalists in Europe is denied, knowing not the occult teachings. They argue that the idea of Boundless Time, as the source of Ahura-Mazdâo, is founded on a grammatical blunder, instead of its being, as it is, an attempt to convey the occult truth of the One Existence, unknowable to human faculties. But although they contest it, they admit the antiquity of the teaching; they must admit that the testimony of ancient days is at one with the occult teaching. If we take the Greek evidence, it speaks with no uncertain voice as to what was taught. Plutarch says: "Cromasdes [Ahura-Mazdâo] sprang

[1] *Gâthâ Ahunavaitî*, trans. by Dr. Haug.

[2] *Op. cit.*, vii. *Qarsêt Nyâyis*, 1 Spiegel.

out of the purest light;"[1] Damascius writes: "The Magi and the whole Áryan nation consider, as Eudemos writes, some Space, and others Time, as the universal cause, out of which the good god as well as the evil spirit were separated, or, as others assert, light and darkness, before these *two spirits arose*."[2] Theodoros speaks of "the nefarious doctrine of the Persians, which Zoroastrades introduced, *viz.*, that about ZOROUAN, whom he makes the ruler of the whole universe, and calls him Destiny; and who, when offering sacrifice in order to generate Hormisdas, produced both Hormisdas and Satan."[3] Very interesting is this blundering account of a controversialist, especially his reference to the occult teaching of the primeval Sacrifice. This again comes out in a "Refutation of Heresies" in the fifth century A.D. by Ezvik: "Before anything, heaven or earth, or creature of any kind whatever therein, was existing, Zeruan existed. . . . He offered sacrifices for a thousand years in the hope of obtaining a son, ORMIZ by name, who was to create heaven, earth, and everything therein."[4] Dr. Haug, who clings to the grammatical-blunder theory, nevertheless acknowledges: "That this doctrine of *Zarvan Akarana* was commonly believed in Persia, during the times of the Sasanians, may be distinctly seen from the reports quoted above (pp. 12–14)."[5] Apart all occult testimony, this is enough to establish that Zarathushtra taught the ancient doctrine of the One Existence,

[1] *Essays on the Parsîs*, p. 9. [2] *Ibid.*, p. 12.
[3] *Ibid.* [4] *Ibid.*, p. 13. [5] *Op. cit.*, pp. 309, 310.

unmanifested, from which the manifested came forth. And when we further read of a primeval sacrifice, performed by God Himself, from which Ahura-Mazdâo was produced, we know by the hint, so dark to the many but so clear to the few, that the primary Sacrifice, the limitation by which manifestation was rendered possible, was also taught by Zarathushtra, as it is known to every student of occultism, and is hinted at over and over again in the Scriptures of the world. H. P. Blavatsky says: "Ahura-Mazda (Asura-Mazda) himself issued from Zeroana Akerna, 'Boundless (circle of) Time,' or the unknown cause. The glory of the latter is too exalted, its light too resplendent for either human intellect or mortal eye to grasp and see. Its primal emanation is eternal light, which, from having been previously concealed in Darkness, was called to manifest itself, and thus was formed Ormazd, the 'King of Life.' He is the 'first-born' in Boundless Time, but like his own antetype (pre-existing spiritual idea) has lived within Darkness from all eternity."[1]

To the occultist, knowing that Zarathushtra was a member of the Brotherhood, there can of course be no doubt as to His teaching on this fundamental truth; but for others the external testimony ought to be sufficient, and the fact that the opposing view is merely the idea of Europeans, ignorant of the ancient lore.

Let us now return to the threefold Ahura-Mazdâo, and His unfolding in order that creation might be.

[1] Article on Zoroastrianism, *Theosophist*, IV., 224.

We learn that from him duality proceeded, Spentô-Mainyush and Angrô-Mainyush, two principles that had their root in Him, but that were unfolded in order that a manifested universe might be brought into existence. The words "good" and "evil" are used to describe these two principles, but they are not the best words of description; the key is given in the most ancient Gâthâs. Good and evil may be said to only come into existence when man in his evolution develops the power of knowledge and of choice; the original duality is not of good and evil, but is of spirit and matter, of reality and non-reality, of light and darkness, of construction and destruction, the two poles between which the universe is woven and without which no universe can be. The second phrase, "reality and non-reality," is used by Zarathushtra Himself in the proclamation of this fundamental truth, for we read in the *Gâthâ Ahunavaitî* that the Prophet declared, standing by the sacred Fire—we will in a few moments see the significance of a declaration made standing by the Fire—"In the beginning there was a pair of twins, two spirits, each of a peculiar activity;" He goes on to say: "And these two spirits united created the first (the material things); one the reality, the other the non-reality."[1] There is that primary duality, Sat and Asat, exactly the occult teaching, that from the One the duality unfolds, in order that the many may proceed. From the One came forth the reality and

[1] *Essays on the Parsîs. Yasna* xxx. 3, 4. Trans. by Dr. Haug.

the unreality. The Prophet goes on to say that the one or the other of these must be followed, of these two "spirits" you must choose one, just as in all ancient teachings it is said that we may choose either spirit or matter; call them, if you will, good and evil, but good and evil are not the fundamental names; it is the spiritual or the material between which the choice of man is made. Various names are given to these two, showing how they were understood in the ancient days. In *Gâthâ Ushatavaitî* (Yasna xlv.) it is said: "All ye who have come from near and far, should now listen and hearken to what I shall proclaim. Now the wise have manifested this universe as a duality. . . . I will proclaim the two primeval spirits of the world, of whom the increaser thus spoke to the destroyer."[1] There are two names again that give us the clue to the secret, the "increaser" and the "destroyer," the one from whom the life is ever pouring forth, and the other the material side, which belongs to form and which is ever breaking up in order that the life may go on into higher expression. As though to impress this on the people, it is said that the so-called evil spirit is the death by which the body of men is struck away; the destruction of form means the passing on of life into higher conditions—not the work of any evil power, but the liberation of the soul, and therefore a part of the divine manifestation of the universe. They are also spoken of as "the two masters," as "the two creators," and we find it declared that the mighty Intelligence

[1] *Op. cit.*, 1, 2.

Srosh worshipped these "two creators who create all things."[1] Surely this great One would not worship evil, though He might reverence the duality in the divine nature. As though to set the question at rest, They are spoken of as "my two spirits" by Ahura-Mazdâo Himself.[2] Dr. Haug fully grasps this idea and remarks: "They are the two moving causes in the universe, united from the beginning, and therefore called 'twins' (*Yémâ*, Sans. *Yaman*). They are present everywhere; in Ahura-Mazda as well as in man. . . . We never find Angro-Mainyush mentioned as a constant opponent of Ahura-Mazda in the Gâthâs, as is the case in later writings. . . . Such is the original Zoroastrian notion of the two creative spirits, who form only two parts of the Divine Being."[3]

A little more difficult, perhaps, to trace, more covered over by a change that came in later times, there is a third person in this primeval Trinity: Ahura-Mazdâo, who is the first and from whom all proceeds; the second, with the duality which is ever the mark of the second Person in the manifested Trinity; the third, the Wisdom, the primeval Wisdom or Mind by which the world was made. This is Armaiti, of whom it is written: "To succor this life (to increase it) Armaiti came with wealth, the good and true mind; she, the everlasting one, created the material world."[4] In later days Armaiti became identified with her creation, and was wor-

[1] *Op. cit.* *Yasna* lvii. 2. [2] *Op. cit.* *Yasna* xix. 9.
[3] *Op. cit.*, pp. 303–305. [4] *Op. cit.* *Gâthâ Ahunavaiti*, 7.

shipped as the Goddess of the earth, but of yore She completed the Trinity.

Next in order come the hierarchies of the heavenly Intelligences, led by the seven great Spirits, the Ameshaspentas, the seven presiding Gods; sometimes Ahura-Mazdâo is placed at Their head as one of Them; sometimes They form the lower septenary and above Them is the higher Triad—a conception familiar to every Theosophist, who knows that the universe is a decade represented by the lower seven and the higher Three, as in the Sephiroth of the Jewish Kabalah. The seven Ameshaspentas, if Ahura-Mazdâo be omitted, are: Vohûman, the Good Mind; Asha Vahishta, the Best Holiness; Khshatraver, Power; Spendarmad, Love; Haurvatât, Health; Ameretâd, Immortality; and Fire, "the most helpful of the Ameshaspentas."[1] To These prayers are continually addressed, hymns are continuually chanted to Them, the whole liturgy is permeated by Their worship; and yet some Oriental scholars—followed in this by only a small minority, I am glad to say, of modern Parsîs—have materialized Them into mere attributes of God, instead of the living Intelligences by whom, as it is said in the Gâthâs, the worlds were made and are sustained.

Dr. Mills degrades Them into mere attributes, and in his translation always thus treats Them, though occasionally forced into very untenable positions by this modern shrinking from the recognition of invisible Intelligences every-

[1] *Yasna* i. 6. Trans. by Spiegel, p. 26.

where. Let us see if They can be taken as mere attributes:

"Yet the most bounteous Mazda Ahura, and Piety with Him,
And Asha the settlements furthering, Thou Good Mind and Thou the Dominion,
Hear ye me, all! and have mercy."[1]

The "qualities" here spelt with capitals are some of the Ameshaspentas, Spendarmad, Vohûman, and Khshatraver, and the plural "ye," as well as the phrase, "hear ye me, *all!*" is a curious way of addressing a God and His qualities.

"Doctrines, Ahura, and actions, tell me which are the best ones, Mazda,
And the debtor's prayer of the praisers; tell me this with the Truth and the Good Mind,
And by Sovereign Power and grace bring on this world's perfection."

The Pahlavi has "Do Thou, therefore, O Aûharmazd, declare to me that which is the best word and deed, and, do ye give that which is Thy debt, O Vohûman, and Thine, O Ashavahist, for this praise, for through your sovereignty, O Aûharmazd, the completion of Progress is made manifestly real in the world at will."[2]

"Thus I conceived Thee, bounteous, Ahura-Mazda,
When with the Good Mind's help obedience neared me,

[1] Gâthâ (*Yas.* xxxiii,) 11. Trans. by Dr. Mills, p. 127.
[2] *Op. cit.*, pp. 152, 153.

And asked of me 'Who art Thou? Whence
thy coming?"[1]

—a curious proceeding for a quality.

"These your favors first ask I thou, Ahura! Asha! and Grant too thine, Áramaiti!"[2]

Many more passages might be cited from the Gâthâs did space permit. Then take this, from the *Yasna haptanhaiti*, admittedly one of the oldest parts of the *Yasna*, after the Gâthâs: "We worship Ahura-Mazda the righteous, master of righteousness. We worship the Ameshaspentas (the archangels), the possessors of good, the givers of good. We worship the whole creation of the righteous spirit."[3] The *Vispered* begins: "I invoke and proclaim to: the Lords of the Heavenly, the Lords of the Earthly,"[4] and so on through a long list of Gods. Again: "We make them known: To Ahura-Mazda, to the holy Sraôsha, to Rashnu the most righteous, to Mithra with large pastures. To the Ameshaspentas, to the Fravarshis of the pure, to the souls of the pure, to the fire, the son of Ahura-Mazda, and to the great lord."[5] The *Yasna* bears its testimony: "I invoke and proclaim to: the creator Ahura-Mazda, the Brilliant, Majestic, Greatest, Best, most Beautiful, the Strongest, most Intellectual, of the best body, the Highest through holiness; who is very wise, who rejoices afar, who created us, who formed us, who keeps us, the Holiest among the

[1] *Ibid.*, p. 165. [2] *Ibid.*, p. 343. [3] *Essays on the Parsîs*, p. 171. [4] *Op. cit.* 1. Trans. by Prof. Spiegel, p. 5. [5] *Ibid.*, xii. 18, 19, p. 18.

heavenly. I invoke and proclaim to: Vohûmano, Ashavahista, Kshathra-Vairya, Spenta-ârmaiti, Haurvat and Ameritât; the body of the cow, the soul of the cow, the fire (the son) of Ahura-Mazda, the most helpful of the Ameshaspentas."[1]

But the *Yasnas* are full of worship, that of the highest Gods, of Mithra,[2] of the Goddess of the waters,[3] of Srosh[4]—one of the mightiest of the great Intelligences—of the sun, moon, and stars.[5] In fact, the whole fabric of Zoroastrianism must be destroyed, if the worship of the Gods is to be wrenched out of it in deference to European materialism. In it, as in Hinduism, the Gods are everywhere, and as the worshipper ascends he worships loftier and loftier Intelligences, till he reaches Ahura-Mazdâo, of whose will they are the agents, by whose life they are sustained.

We now come to the Fire, the supreme symbol of God, the symbol of divine life, that which is called the Son of Ahura-Mazdâo, the sacred symbol most reverenced by the Zoroastrians of to-day. As we might expect, we find prayer after prayer addressed to the Fire, worship addressed to the Fire in the plainest, the clearest, and the most explicit terms, the Fire which is declared to be the most helpful of all the spiritual intelligences, the Fire which is

[1] *Yasna* i. 1–6. Trans. by Prof. Spiegel, p. 26.
[2] *Mihir Yasht. Essays on the Parsis*, p. 202.
[3] *Abân Yasht. Ibid.*, p. 197.
[4] *Yasna* lvii. *Ibid.*, p. 189.
[5] *Yasna* iv. 39. Trans. by Spiegel, p. 42.

the most friendly, coming down from Ahura-Mazdâo and acquainted with all heavenly secrets. "Happy is the man to whom thou comest mightily, Fire, son of Ahura-Mazda. More friendly than the most friendly, more worthy of adoration than the most worthy of honor. Mayest thou come helpfully to us at the greatest business. Fire, thou art acquainted with Ahura-Mazda, acquainted with the heavenly. Thou art the holiest of the same (the fire) that bears the name Vâzista. O Fire, son of Ahura-Mazda, we draw near to thee."[1]

What is the Fire? Ever, in every religion, has fire been the symbol of the supreme God; Brahman is fire; Ahura-Mazdâo is fire; the Jews worship their God as a pillar of fire, and the Christians proclaim, "Our God is a consuming fire." Everywhere fire has been and is the supreme emblem; for He who is glory is revealed as fire; it blazes out from That which "is dark by excess of light," and the whole universe is but the outcome of the living flame. Oh! if I could show you Zarathushtra, the mighty One, as He first spake to the people, and taught them the truths that the Fire had revealed to Him, the Sons of the Fire who sent Him to the earth to teach those truths to the people. Picture Him standing by the altar, speaking of what the Fire revealed to Him. Remember what is said in one of those "Oracles" which reproduce the early traditions: "When thou beholdest a sacred Fire, formless, flashing dazzlingly throughout the world, Hear thou the

[1] *Yasna* XXXVI., ii. 4–10. Trans. by Prof. Spiegel, p. 96.

voice of the Fire." As Zarathushtra spake there was at first no fire at the altar at his side; there was sandalwood in fragrant heaps, there were perfumes, but no fire. As the prophet stood there He held a Rod—of which every occultist knows, a Rod, a copy of which was used in the Mysteries—filled with the living fire of the upper spheres, and with the twining fire-serpents round it. As he raised that Rod, pointing it to heaven, through infinite space, through the vault of the blue sky, the heavens burst into fire, and lambent flames played on every side; cleaving the air, some of these flames darted downwards and fired the altar at His side, and the living fire wreathing round Him made Him a mass of flame as He spake "the Words of the Fire," and proclaimed the everlasting truths. That was how Zarathushtra taught in the ancient days. And He gave the hymns of fire, that could call it down from above—the compelling mantras, the words of power—and century after century, millennium after millennium, the fire that blazed on the Zoroastrian altar in the fire-temple was no mere mingling of material flames. Ever from above, from the heavens, the sacred fire was called down from the fiery Ákâsha; at the word of the priest, that fell upon the altar and there blazed as the living symbol of God. When the lower priesthood had to act, when the higher one was not available for the service, then they were given the rod of fire in which the electric fire was ever flashing, the living flame, and as they touched the altar-fuel with that rod the heavenly fire blazed out.

Even now, see how the tradition has come down, in the very ceremonies by which the fire is lighted on the new altar. To-day there is still a faint echo of the ancient truth, although the power has departed and no Parsî Dastur can summon fire from on high. Fire is gathered from all the different sources in the town wherein the sacred flame is to be lighted, but the fire is not used as it is gathered from the earthly fuel; for the officiator places above the gathered fire an iron tray heaped with sandalwood, and holding it high above, so that material contact shall not be, the fire below lights the fuel, and a second fire leaps up; nine times over that ceremony is repeated, until the very essence of fire, as it were, is gathered—pure for the pure, and worthy to be the symbol of the divine. Further, they seek to have the electric fire, the fire of lightning, flashing down from heaven, and, as they are now unable to call it down for themselves, sometimes even for years they have to wait before that last fire is gathered, sometimes for years are patient ere that fire may be mingled with the others that burn upon the sacred altar. Before that sacred Fire every Zoroastrian bows, and in the Zoroastrian home, when sunset falls, a fragrant fire is carried through every room in the gathering dusk, emblem of the purifying, the protecting power of the Supreme.

We must now hastily glance at the way in which man is regarded, that we may understand his place in the hierarchy of Intelligences. In him are the two principles—spirit and matter—as in all else, and he can side with the one or the other. All the ethic is based on the idea that he shall throw himself on the side of the pure, battle for the pure, maintain the pure. It may be that the latter view of Angrô-Mainyush as the enemy was an attempt to stir man into active conflict against evil, to make him feel he was fighting the battle of the "good spirit" against the "evil spirit." To be in everything actively on the side of purity is a personal duty. The Zoroastrian must keep the earth pure, must till it as a religious duty; he must perform all the functions of agriculture as a service to the Gods, for the earth is the pure creature of Ahura-Mazdâo, to be guarded from all pollution. The air must be kept pure. The water must be kept pure; if anything unclean, like a corpse, falls into the water, the good Zoroastrian must remove it, that the pure element may not be fouled. Hence also the objection to burning a dead body, as polluting the fire by the touch of the unclean. Therefore is the body reverently carried to the Towers of Silence, and in that guarded place, open but to the heavens, it is laid, that the vultures may swiftly devour it, and no pure element may thereby be soiled.

Passing from that purity of eternal nature with which a Parsî must not only passively but also actively associate himself, we come to that famous axiom of their religion: "Pure thoughts, pure words, pure deeds." That is the constantly reiterated rule of the Zoroastrian life—and we notice that the three are placed in the occult order—repeated in his daily prayers, insisted on at every turn. The first words of the *Khordah Avesta* form the Ashem-Vohû, the most sacred formula daily repeated: "Purity is the best good. Happiness, happiness is to him—namely, to the best pure in purity."[1] When Ashura-Mazdâo is answering Zarathushtra as to the recital of the Ashem-Vohû, He declares that the recital of the Ashem-Vohû that is worth all the good things created by Himself is "when one forsakes evil thoughts and evil words and evil deeds."[2]

Between the ages of seven and fifteen, the child must be initiated, and then is put on him (or her) for the first time the kusti, or sacred thread, and the sûdrâ, or white linen shirt, both emblems of purity. The kusti is made of seventy-two threads of lambs-wool, and is wound thrice round the waist, signifying the good thoughts, words, and deeds incumbent on the wearer; it is knotted twice in front and twice behind. Truthfulness, chastity, obedience to parents, hospitality, industry, honesty, kindness to useful animals, are virtues on which special stress is laid, and charity is made an essential part of religion. It is to be wise charity and bestowed on the deserving; especially are recommended helping the poor, helping those to marry who cannot afford to do so, helping to educate the children of those unable to perform this duty for themselves. Ervad Sheriarji Dadabhai Barucha says: "Just as certain virtues are

[1] *Op. cit.* Translated by Prof. Spiegel, p. 3.
[2] *Hadokht Nask. Essays on the Parsîs*, p. 219.

said to be the peculiar attributes of the four classes of the people, and highly becoming to them, so certain vices are specially to be shunned by them. For the priestly class hypocrisy, covetousness, negligence, slothfulness, attention to trifles, and unbelief in religion are peculiarly unbecoming. The warrior must be above oppression, violence, breach of promise, encouragement of evil, ostentation, arrogance, and insolence. The husbandman must fly from ignorance, envy, ill-will, and malice; and the artisan must avoid incredulity, ingratitude rudeness, and slander (Mainyo-i Khart, LIX.)."[1] It is interesting to notice that when Ahura-Mazdâo proclaimed "the righteous" (Ahuna-Vairya) both spiritual and earthly, the Ahuna-Vairya had three lines—the four classes, the five chiefs, and a conclusion. The classes were the fourfold order of priests, warriors, agriculturists, and artizans,[2] another mark of the close kinship of the Iranians with the first Âryan sub-race.

Other of these marks are interesting: the sacrifice of the Homa, worshipped as fervently and extolled as highly in the *Homa Yasht*[3] as in the *Sama Veda;* the names of the priests—the Âtharva (Atharvan), the Zaota (Hotâ), and the identity by function of the Rathwi with the Adhvârya; milk, ghee, holy water, sacred twigs, are all used in certain ceremonies; Parsîs, like Hindus, have their prayers for the dead, at stated intervals. In truth, the two faiths are

[1] *Zoroastrian Religion and Customs*, p. 31.

[2] *Yasna*, XIX. 17. *Essays on the Parsîs*, p. 188.

[3] *Essays on the Parsîs*, pp. 176–185.

sister faiths, only invasion, oppression, and exile have shattered the younger faith to such an extent that much of its ancient birthright has been lost.

The seven principles of the human constitution are clearly mentioned in *Yasna* LIV. 1: "Bodies together with bones, vital power and form, strength and consciousness, soul and Fravarshi."[1] The first three are the dense and etheric bodies with Prâna; strength is Kamâ, consciousness is Manas, Urvan (translated soul) is Buddhi, and Fravarshi is Âtmâ. "Every being of the good creation, whether living or deceased, or still unborn, has its own Fravarshi," says Dr. Haug.[2] But this hardly gives the full idea of the word, as it is expounded in the *Fravardin Yasht*, in which Ahura-Mazdâo declares that everything good is maintained by their splendor and glory. They are called the "strong guardian-angels of the righteous," and evidently represent the Âtmâ, and in many cases the Âtmâ when Manas and Buddhi have been merged in it.

After death, the soul passes into the intermediate world, "the time-worn paths which are for the wicked and which are for the righteous,"[3] spoken of by Ahura-Mazdâo as "the frightful, deadly, destructive path which is the separation of the body and soul,"[4] Kâmaloka. The soul of the righteous meets

[1] *Op. cit.* Translated by Prof. Spiegel, p. 120.

[2] *Essays on the Parsis*, p. 206.

[3] *Vendidad*, Fargard. XIX. 29. *Essays on the Parsis*, p. 255.

[4] *Hadokht Nask*, Yt. XXII. 17. *Ibid.*, p. 222.

a beautiful maiden, the embodiment of his good thoughts, good words, and good deeds; he crosses the "bridge of the judge" safely, and reaches heaven. But the soul of the wicked meets a hideous hag, the embodiment of his evil thoughts, evil words, and evil deeds, and he fails to cross the bridge and falls into fire.

Again much is left untold, much is too briefly, too baldly described; yet enough has been said to justify the occultist when he bears witness to this ancient religion, the second of the Fifth Race religions, that it springs from the primeval source, that its Prophet was one of the Divine Initiates, that it comes down from the past, millennium after millennium, and is but poorly represented by the comparatively materialized Zoroastrianism of to-day. The study of its Scriptures might revive it; the old knowledge might again be breathed into it; these concessions to European criticism and European materialism might be repudiated by every Zoroastrian as no part of his ancient, of his glorious faith. O my Parsî brothers! your Prophet is not dead. He is not perished: He is watching over the religion that He founded, ever seeking to raise it from its present degradation, to give it back its lost knowledge, its lost powers. What nobler work for the Zoroastrian of to-day than to permeate his brethren with the ancient Fire, to relight its blaze on the spiritual altar of their hearts? What nobler work than to study his own Scriptures, and to go forth and teach the ancient learning with the authority and power that can only be wielded by a man of the same faith with those he addresses? The Fire is not dead; it is only smouldering on its ancient altars; white-hot are the ashes, ready to reburst into flames. And I dream of a day when the breath of the great Prophet Zarathushtra shall sweep again through His temples, fanning the ashes on the altars of those ancient fanes, and every altar shall flash into fire, and again from heaven the answering flames shall fall, making the Iranian religion once more what it ought to be, a beacon-light for the souls of men, one of the greatest religions of the world.

BUDDHISM.

BROTHERS, as you well know, the religion known as Buddhism is the religion which has the largest number of adherents in the world. Despite all difficulties of accurate statistics, we may take it that about one-third of the human race follow the teachings of the Buddha, and in Europe a very large amount of attention has been drawn to these teachings by the devoted work of a number of Orientalists who have been fascinated by the charm of the Buddha Himself, by the purity, by the elevation of His teachings. For many reasons into which I cannot now go in detail, Buddhism has greater attraction for the European mind than either Hinduism or Zoroastrianism—Buddhism especially in the form in which it is taught in the southern Church. The northern Church—Buddhism as it is found in Tibet and China—is so closely allied to Hinduism in its teaching as to the Gods, as to the continuing Ego, as to the life after death, as to rites and ceremonies, as to the use of Sanskrit mantras, that it has less attraction for the European. For you must remember that the European has a mind which is essentially practical rather than metaphysical, and that he is inclined to be repulsed by much talk about the invisible world and by much teaching which refers to the more mystic side of religion. In the southern Church this mystic side in course of time has apparently disapppeared, to a very great extent at least, so far as the translations are concerned that the Europeans possess. Books which deal with the more mystic side are not yet translated, and therefore are not before the European public. What they recognize as Buddhism is a system of wonderful ethics couched in the most beautiful and in the most poetical language; they recognize in it these moral teachings coupled with rare liberality of thought, with the constant appeal to the reason, with the constant attempt to justify and render intelligible the foundations on which the morals are built; and this appeals very strongly to the minds of many Europeans, who have turned aside from the cruder presentments of religion that are current in Europe, and who seek in Buddhism a refuge from the complete scepticism to which otherwise they would feel themselves doomed.

Now with regard to the teachings of Buddhism, I shall found myself on the Buddhist Scriptures themselves, for that is the fairest way of dealing with a faith; and then, as always, looking at these in the light of occult knowledge, I shall try to show you how consistent they are with the noblest teachings of other faiths, with the essential truths of religion, and how it is very largely owing to misconception, to misrepresentation, to the small extent, we may say, to which some of the later disciples have expounded the teachings of the Buddha—it is largely in consequence of these misconceptions and omissions that in the land which was His birthplace, amongst the people to whom by race He belonged, His doctrines are now looked upon with so much of suspicion, and scarcely any are found to accept His teachings or willing to call themselves by His name. Daughter of Hinduism Buddhism most undoubtedly is, daughter of the ancient faith, born in comparatively modern times, and if rightly read the Buddhist Scriptures are the echo of the Hindu Scriptures, and the teachings—though often thrown into a less metaphysical and a more directly practical form—are teachings that are penetrated with the Hindu spirit, as indeed you might expect, remembering the lips that spake them. The form into which they were thrown is specially adapted for spreading these truths outside the limits of India itself, a form which by the foreknowledge of the Buddha was made to carry the teachings of the purest Hindu morality into many a country outside the limits within which Hinduism would be taught, intended to spread it through populations less keenly metaphysical and less intellectual than those of the Hindu people. We find here, as I say, the fundamental verities, though the form into which they are thrown is simpler and is in many ways perhaps more directly practical. The mission of the Buddha—while it began in India with the hope perchance that the whole work might go on in harmony and without disruption—was intended to carry the light of truth to other peoples, a mission that has been triumphantly fulfilled, and that, we may hope, will continue to be fulfilled for many an age to come.

Now the essential teachings of the Buddha are contained in the three great divisions of Buddhist sacred literature, the three Pitakas, or baskets, as they are called. The first of these is the Vinâya, and contains all the rules laid down for the monastic order that He established, the famous Sangha, the guardian and repository of His religion. In addition to the rules of discipline, we have also in this Vinâya a large number of teachings given by the Buddha, more mystical in their character than those of some of the other volumes; being specially intended for the training of the monastic order, specially intended for the teaching of the disciples, these books speak out more plainly as to the invisible world than do some others; they give out more fully what is regarded by the materializing West as the legendary side of Buddhism; but this is really a true and essential part of Buddhist teaching, and, as was said long afterwards, by Nagarjuna: "'Every Buddha has both a revealed and a mystic doctrine.' The exoteric is for the multitude of new disciples. The esoteric is for the Bodhisattvas and advanced pupils, such as Kâshiapa. It is not communicated in the form of definite language, and could not, therefore, be transmitted by Ánanda, as definite doctrine among the Sûtras. Yet it is virtually contained in the Sûtras. For instance, the *Fa-hwa-king*, or 'Sûtra of the Lotus of the Good Law,' which is regarded as containing the cream of the revealed doctrine, is to be viewed as a sort of original document of the esoteric teaching, while it is in form exoteric."[1] When the Buddha was seventy-one years of age He expounded the esoteric doctrine in answer to the questions put to Him by His great disciple Kâshiapa, and although, as Mr. Edkins says, this doctrine could not be fully put into language—for always the esoteric doctrine, being spiritual, is beyond intellectual language—none the less can it be deduced from the Sûtras. The second of these three Pitakas consists of Sûtras, or Suttas, as they are generally called—because the Buddha is supposed to have spoken in Prakrit, the common dialect derived from Sanskrit, which it is now called Pâli. The Suttas form that part of the Buddha's teachings which were given to the people, His ethical teachings, and discussions, disputations, questionings, explanations arising out of them and out of circumstances that He met with in His daily life. Here are the great records of the life and teachings of the Buddha, showing that life as it was lived in India, and those teachings as they fell from His sacred lips. The third Pitaka is the Abhidhamma, of which very little is known at present in the West. It is said to be full of mysticism, and to contain the Buddhist philosophy as apart from the Buddhist ethics. But that I must leave on one side, as unreachable by us, and there is plenty of matter in the other two Pitakas to take up very much more than all the time at our disposal.[2]

[1] *Chinese Buddhism*, by Rev. J. Edkins, p. 43.

[2] Dr. Rhys Davids says: "The books, as we have them, were

In considering how I should lay this great teaching before you, what would be the form which would make it at once most attractive and most instructive, I decided that it would be best to put it in the way that we may say it originally came to the people who listened to the Buddha Himself, for His teaching is so interwoven with His life, its beauty and its fascination depend so largely on the One who uttered it and on the marvellous perfection of that many-sided life, that to describe it as a mere dry system, apart from the life of the Blessed One, seems to deprive it of its inspiring force, to deprive it of its greatest influence over the lives of men.

Let me remind you, at the very outset, of the way in which the Buddha is looked upon, alike by His own disciples, by every occultist, and by every one who knows anything of the invisible world and of the way in which the position of a Buddha is gained. Many a hundred incarnations went before that final incarnation in which the illumination of the Buddha was attained. Step by step He climbed up the long

put into their present shape in the century or two after the death of Gotama" (*Buddhism*). At the Council of Râjagriha, under Kâshiapa and Ánanda, held immediately after the death of the Buddha, "Buddhism" may be said to have been organized. At the second Council, that of Vaishâli, under Yashas and Revata, held 377 B.C., the dissentients rejected the Abhidhamma, but the disputes it was called to settle were merely on certain points in the discipline of the Sangha. The third Council, under Ashoka, at Pâtaliputta in B.C. 242, again left the Pitakas unchallenged, so that we may fairly take them as representing accurately the doctrines of the great Teacher.

ladder of existence; life after life of self-sacrifice and devotion led Him from earthly manhood to divine humanity, from divine humanity to the position of a Bodhisattva, from the position of a Bodhisattva to that of a Buddha. The Buddha is said to have perfected His vow kalpa after kalpa. Immeasurable ages of innumerable lives lay behind Him ere He was born in the town of Kalpilavastu, in the palace of the king, born for His last birth upon this planet, born to reach the perfect illumination, and to become one of the series of supreme Teachers of Gods and men. In the Valley of the Ganges, about a hundred miles to the northeast of the sacred city of Benares, this child was born, and it is said, and truly said, that all nature rejoiced over His birth-hour, knowing the work He had come to accomplish in the world. It is said that Devas showered flowers on the mother and the child, that the rejoicing shook all the worlds of Gods and men, for the child that was born was to be a mighty Teacher, the instructor of myriads and myriads of the human race. The date of His birth is put by the Sinhalese at B.C. 623; at B.C. 685 by the Siamese.[1] He was named by His parents Siddhartha, "He who has accomplished His purpose"; that name was given because of a prophecy made by a great Brâhmana soon after His birth, that the child should be a mighty teacher and an enlightener of the nations of the earth. He grew up during His youth apparently in ignorance of His mighty destiny. It is a

[1] Dr. Rhys Davids says it "may be fixed approximately at about B.C. 600." *Buddhism*, p. 20.

strange problem that has pressed on many minds how it is that, with some of the greatest who are born into the world, the knowledge of their own greatness is for a time veiled. You may remember it was the same with Râma. He did not in His early days show any knowledge that He was an Avatâra of the Supreme; He was taught by Vasishta, and from him received in His then body the knowledge of true Yoga. So also with the Buddha; as we trace Him through the beautiful life he led as a boy, as a youth, up to the date of his marriage with his cousin, and for still a year or two afterwards, we see him leading indeed a noble, a beautiful, and a pure life, but a life that did not apparently recognize its own greatness, with the mind turned to the invisible world but not yet realizing its mission nor the part it had to play. We read how His father, longing that He should be the king of earth rather than the monarch over millions of minds of men in the spiritual world, tried to keep back from Him the knowledge of the suffering that was going on in the world around. He environed Him on all sides with all that was fair and delightful, in order that the knowledge of the sorrow of the world might be shut out from His eyes. We read how by the guiding of a Deva He was led to go forth from His palace and the pleasure-garden that surrounded it, and driving in His chariot He met four men who gave Him the first touch of the awakening. First, He met a man who was aged, and up till this time He had never seen but the young; He asked what was this man, half-blind, tottering, and palsied, with a wrinkled face, with weakness in every limb; and His charioteer answered, he was an aged man, and that to all that were born into the world age must come in time. He met a man suffering from horrible disease; He had seen nothing but health and beauty, and He asked what was this; the charioteer told him, this is disease, under which many of the children of men must suffer. He met a corpse, He who had seen nothing but the living, and He asked what was this; and the charioteer said, it is death, to which all who are living must come. And lastly He met an ascetic, calm, serene, and peaceful, full of happiness, full of peace, and He asked how it was that in a world where there were old age, disease and death this man could thus walk serene. He was answered that this man had a life beyond the life of men, a life fixed in the eternal; hence his peace, his serenity, his calm in the midst of sorrow. And going back to His palace the prince reflected, and from His lips broke forth the cry: "Full of hindrance is this household life, the haunt of passion; free as the air is the homeless state." That idea fastened on Him —the contrast between the haunt of passion and the homeless man; until at last, rising in the night when wife and child were sleeping beside Him, He bent over the young wife, beautiful in her sleep, and over the babe that lay beside her in the first tenderness of its youth, and touching them not, lest He should awaken them and their cry should shake His purpose, He went forth from the palace of His father, called

His faithful charioteer to bring His horse, and went through the silent sleeping city, through the quiet streets of the deserted town, until, coming to the gates of the city, He dismounted from His horse, gave it to the charioteer and bade him lead it back to the palace, stripped off His princely garments, cut off His hair, and went forth alone, homeless, to seek for the cause of human sorrow and for its cure. He who was to be the Buddha could not live in joy and happiness in the palace of the king, while men outside were suffering, were agonizing, and were dying; He went out to seek the cause of the suffering, and the cure which He might bring to human woe.

Then we trace Him in the search He made after divine wisdom. First going to great recluses, to Alâra Kâlamâ, and Uddaka, He tried to learn from them the secret; they were learned in philosophy, in religion, and He sought to learn from them the cause and the cure of sorrow. He studied the mysteries of philosophy, He sat at their feet learning all the intricacies of metaphysics, and at last despairing He arose, feeling that not there was the cure of sorrow, not by mere intellectual learning should the salvation of men be found. Going onwards, He met five ascetics, and for six years He gave Himself to the ascetic life, practising penances greater than any other practised, reducing His food at last to a mere grain a day, until finally He fell, emaciated, fainting and helpless, worn out by the rigor of His austerities. A passing girl, Nanda, brought Him rice and milk; He took the food and arose refreshed, and when His comrades saw that He had taken food they turned from Him, saying, "This ascetic is going back to the world, he is weary of austerity, and is unworthy of the sacred vocation." And they left him, and again He went forth alone, to find in solitude the secret of human woe.

As He was wandering on His way, the time approached when illumination was to be found, and, reaching Gâya, He sat down beneath the sacred Asvattha tree, saying that He would never rise from His seat until light had dawned upon His spirit and the secret of sorrow was found. He sat there patiently, and all the hosts of Mâra, the evil ones, assailed Him with temptations of pleasure and with threats of pain; all the Asuras gathered round Him, seeking to shake His constancy and to modify his determination. He sat clad in the garment of pure resolution, untouched, unshaken, even when the image of His weeping wife appeared before Him, with outstretched arms pleading that He would turn His face backward to the world again. At last in the silent hour the illumination came. As He sat beneath the sacred tree, there dawned on Him the light which He had been born into the world to discover; there came to Him that mighty awakening which made Him the Enlightened, the Buddha, which told Him of sorrow, of the cause of sorrow, of the cure of sorrow, of the path which leads beyond it; Buddhahood was achieved, a Saviour of the world was there. And then there breaks from His lips the song triumphant, that must be familiar to many amongst you: "Looking for the maker of this tabernacle, I shall have to run through a course of many births, so long as I do not find (him); and painful is birth again and again. But now, maker of the tabernacle, thou hast been seen; thou shalt not make up this tabernacle again. All thy rafters are broken, thy ridge-pole is sundered; the mind, approaching the Eternal, has attained to the extinction of all desires."[1]

That was the secret of the Buddha—that by the extinction of desires man rose to peace. Under the tree of wisdom He had seen the sorrow of the world, its cause in desire, its end in the ending of desire, and the noble eight-fold path which led out of it into peace eternal. Seeing it for Himself and for the race, He passed into Nirvâna, the uncreated, the passionless, the all-embracing. And when the Blessed One had thus entered into Nirvâna, He sat beneath the Bodhi tree for seven days, "enjoying the bliss of emancipation."[2]

During the night closing the seventh day, He "fixed His mind upon the chain of causation" and traced the evolution of the universe, expressing it

[1] *Dhammapada*, 153, 154. Sacred Books of the East, vol. x., translated by Max Müller.

[2] *Mahâvagga*, I., i. 1. The account of this period may be read in the Sacred Books of the East, vol. xiii., *Vinâya Texts*, translated from the Pâli by Drs. Rhys Davids and Oldenburg. Or, as regards the teaching of the Bhikkhus, it will be found in vol. xi., *Buddhist Suttas*, translated by Dr. Rhys Davids, in *Dhamma-Kakkha-Ppavattana-Sutta*.

in the twelve Nidânas, the succession of which shows the order of the stages, until we reach the suffering we find around us; the first is Avidyâ, "ignorance," *i.e.*, limitation, the primary cause—because without this limitation in All-Consciousness, by the action of the Supreme, no universe, no variety, can arise. From Avidyâ come the Samkhâras, from these Consciousness, then Name and Form, then the six Powers of Perception, from these Contact, from Contact Sensation, from Sensation Desire, from Desire Attachment, from Attachment "Existence"—*i.e.*, personality—from this Birth, and from Birth Decay with all the sorrows of life.[1] These form the evolutionary chain, and properly understood and unfolded contain the whole philosophy of the evolving universe and its returning path.

Arising from His seat under the Bodhi tree, the Buddha sat under a banyan tree for another seven days, at the end of which, in answer to a Brâhmana, He spoke words that explain His whole attitude to Brâhmanas: "That Brâhmana who has removed (from himself) all sinfulness, who is free from haughtiness, free from impurity, self-restrained, who is an accomplished master of knowledge (or of the Veda), who has fulfilled the duties of holiness, such a Brâhmana may justly call himself a Brâhmana, whose behavior is uneven to nothing in the world."[2]

For two more periods of seven days each the Buddha sat under two other trees, and then He took

[1] *Ibid.*, 2. [2] *Ibid.*, ii. 2.

food from two merchants, who became His first disciples. Returning to His seat under the banyan tree, a strange scene occurred. "In the mind of the Blessed One, who was alone, and had retired into solitude, the following thought arose: 'I have penetrated this doctrine which is profound, difficult to perceive and to understand, which brings quietude of heart, which is exalted, which is unattainable by reasoning, abstruse, intelligible (only) to the wise.'[1] This people, on the other hand, is given to desire, intent upon desire, delighting in desire. To this people, therefore, who are given to desire, intent upon desire, delighting in desire, the law of causality and the chain of causation will be a matter difficult to understand; most difficult for them to understand will be also the extinction of all samkhâras, the getting rid of all the substrata of (existence), the destruction of desire, the absence of passion, quietude of heart, Nirvâna. Now if I proclaim the doctrine, and other men are not able to understand my preaching, there would result but weariness and annoyance to me.' And then the following . . . stanzas, unheard before, occurred to the Blessed One: 'With great pains have I acquired it. Enough! Why should I now proclaim it? The doctrine will not be easy to understand to beings that are lost in lust and hatred. Given to lust, surrounded with thick darkness, they will not see what is repugnant (to

[1] Yet people fancy that Buddhism is a simple ethical system, founded wholly on reason, and capable of being grasped in its entirety by the unspiritual!

their minds), abstruse, profound, difficult to perceive and subtle.' "[1]

At this crisis Brahmâ Sahampati (the third Logos of our chain) intervened, seeing that "the mind of the Tathâgata, of the holy, of the absolute Sambuddha inclines itself to remain in quiet, and not to preach the doctrine." He tells the Buddha that some will understand and reminds Him of the suffering earth: "Look down, all-seeing One, upon the people lost in suffering, overcome by birth and decay, Thou who hast freed thyself from suffering! Arise, O hero, O victorious One! Wander through the world, O Leader of the pilgrim band,[2] who Thyself art free from debt. May the Blessed One preach the doctrine; there will be people who can understand it!" And so He looked on the world, with the eye of a Buddha, full of compassion, and saying: "Wide open is the door of the Immortal to all who have ears to hear; let them send forth faith to meet it. The Dhamma sweet and good I spake not, Brahmâ, despairing of the weary task, to men."[3]

He then arose, and whither did he go, to commence His beneficent mission? He went to the sacred city whence spiritual missions have ever started in India; he went to Kâshî, to the holy spot whence the spiritual life of India has ever taken its rise; and there in Isipatana, in the deer park of the city of Benares, He set rolling the wheel of the Law.

[1] *Ibid.*, v. 2, 3.
[2] The hosts of reincarnating Egos, held in debt by Karma.
[3] *Ibid.*, 4-10.

Here were dwelling the five ascetics who had turned their backs on Him. To them He went, and, announcing Himself as Sambuddha, He told them that the two extremes of self-indulgence and of constant self-mortification were alike profitless, and that, avoiding these, He had trodden "the middle path, which leads to insight, which leads to wisdom, which conduces to calm, to knowledge, to the sambodhi,[1] to Nirvâna." This middle path is the holy or noble eightfold path, the fourth of the "Four Noble Truths." It is Right Belief, Right Aspiration, Right Speech, Right Conduct, Right Livelihood, Right Endeavor, Right Memory, Right Meditation. He then expounded to them the other three Truths He had seen under the Bodhi tree: "This, O Bhikkhus, is the Noble Truth of Suffering: Birth is suffering; decay is suffering; illness is suffering; death is suffering; presence of objects we hate is suffering; separation from objects we love is suffering; not to obtain what we desire is suffering. Briefly, the fivefold clinging[2] to existence is suffering. This, O Bhikkhus, is the Noble Truth of the cause of suffering: Thirst, that leads to rebirth, accompanied by pleasure and lust, finding its delights here and there. (This thirst is threefold), namely, thirst for pleasure, thirst for existence, thirst for prosperity. This, O Bhikkhus, is the Noble Truth of the cessation of suffering: (it ceases with) the complete cessation of

[1] All-knowledge.

[2] Clinging to the five elements of existence which make the transitory self, the five sheaths.

this thirst—a cessation which consists in the absence of every passion—with the abandoning of this thirst, with the doing away with it, with the deliverance from it, with the destruction of desire." When the "supreme wheel of the empire of Truth" was thus set rolling, it is recorded that all the Devas, beginning with those of the earth and passing to the seventh or highest, world, shouted with joy, and cried that none could ever again turn back the wheel.[1] Yet further He explained to them the difference between the Self and the not-Self, in words that should forever have made impossible the contention that He taught that there was no continuing life in man: "The body (rûpa), O Bhikkhus, is not the self. . . . Sensation, O Bhikkhus, is not the self. . . . Perception is not the self. . . . The Samkhâras are not the Self. . . . Consciousness is not the self." Defining each more fully, He declares of each that it "is not mine, is not me, is not my Self, thus it should be remembered by right knowledge according to the truth." And He concludes: "Considering this, O Bhikkhus, a learned, noble hearer of the word becomes weary of body, weary of sensation, weary of perception, weary of the Samkhâras, weary of consciousness. Becoming weary of all that, he divests himself of passion: by absence of passion he is made free; when he is free, he becomes aware that he is free; and he realizes

[1] The absurd modern idea that a Buddha could deny the existence of the Gods had not then been born, and all the early records are full of their co-operation and rejoicings.

that rebirth is exhausted; that holiness is completed: that duty is fulfilled: that there is no further return to this world."[1]

From this time forth, the Lord Buddha preached His doctrine, and men and women became enlightened, obtaining, as He taught, "the pure and spotless Eye of the Truth," the knowledge that all that has a beginning must have an ending; then they surrendered all worldly things and became Bhikkhus, mendicants, putting on the yellow robe, carrying the alms-bowl, taking refuge in the Buddha, in His Law and in His Order. And the Order grew and multiplied, and after a while the Lord sent out His disciples to teach, and gave them authority to admit to the Sangha (the Order) those who sought entrance, on the triple declaration thrice repeated, "I take my refuge in the Buddha. I take my refuge in the Dhamma. I take my refuge in the Sangha."[2]

Dr. Rhys Davids, who is so fascinated by the ethical life of Buddhism—and who so utterly and so strangely resents its inner spirit, and declares that in Buddhist teaching there is no continuing Ego, no development of the eternal and spiritual nature of man—gives us from Buddha Ghosa's commentary on the first of the Dialogues a most attractive pic-

[1] *Ibid.*, vi. Every student will recognize here the koshas of the Vedânta, noting that the Samkhâras represent the Prânamayakosha, sensation and perception the Manomayakosha: the fifth, Anandamayakosha, is not mentioned, for that film of bliss is not lost even in the Turiya state, obtaining which a man returneth not.

[2] *Ibid.*, xii. 3, 41.

ture of the daily round of that holy life. "The Blessed One used to rise up early (*i.e.*, about 5 A.M.), and, out of consideration for his personal attendant, was wont to wash and dress himself, without calling for any assistance. Then, till it was time to go on his round for alms, he would retire to a solitary place and meditate. When that time arrived he would dress himself completely in the three robes (which every member of the Order wore in public), take his bowl in his hand, and, sometimes alone, sometimes attended by his followers, would enter the neighboring village or town for alms, sometimes in an ordinary way, sometimes wonders happening," recounted at length. Then people would come out and pray Him to accept His food from them, and He would sit down and eat. "Then would the Blessed One, when the meal was done, discourse to them, with due regard to their capacity for spiritual things, in such a way that some would take the layman's vow, and some would enter on the paths, and some would reach the highest fruit thereof. And when he had thus had mercy on the multitude, he would arise from his seat and depart to the place where he had lodged. And when he had come there he would sit in the open verandah, awaiting the time when the rest of his followers should also have finished their meal." Then, standing at the door of his room, He would speak a few words of exhortation, and at the request of any disciple would "suggest a subject for meditation, suitable to the spiritual capacity of each." The disciples departing to meditate, the Buddha would rest awhile, and "when his body was rested he would arise from the couch and for a space consider the circumstances of the people near that he might do them good. And at the fall of the day the folk from the neighboring villages or town would gather together at the place where he was lodging, bringing with them offerings of flowers. And to them seated in the lecture-hall would he, in a manner suitable to the occasion, and suitable to their beliefs, discourse of the Truth." Dismissing them, at the close of the day, He would sometimes bathe, and then sit alone, "till the brethren, returned from their meditations, began to assemble. Then some would ask him questions on things that puzzled them, some would speak of their meditations, some would ask for an exposition of the Truth. Thus would the first watch of the night pass, as the Blessed One satisfied the desire of each, and then they would take their leave. And part of the rest of the night would he spend in meditation, walking up and down outside his chamber; and part he would rest lying down, calm and self-possessed within. And as the day began to dawn, rising from his couch he would seat himself, and calling up before his mind the folk in the world, he would consider the aspirations which they, in previous births, had formed and think over the means by which he could help them to attain thereto."[1]

Into the framework of this noble, simple life, the jewels of the Buddha's teachings were set. In order

[1] *Buddhism*, pp. 108–112.

to appreciate them we need to remember this environment, to remember that the Buddha was a Hindu speaking to Hindus on matters largely familiar to them, using religious and metaphysical terms in their ordinary accepted meanings, raising no opposition as a heretic—as He assuredly would have done had His teaching been materialistic, as it became later among some non-Hindus, ignorant of the connotation of the terms employed—a Teacher, distinguishable by His contemporaries from other teachers of His time only by the incomparable purity, compassion, and wisdom that breathed from His every look, His every word. Dr. Rhys Davids, regarding Buddhism as "diametrically opposed" to Hinduism, regards it as an evidence of wonderful toleration that He was allowed to teach so peacefully. "It is even more than that. Wherever he went, it was precisely the Brahmins themselves who often took the most earnest interest in his speculations, though his rejection of the soul theory and of all that it involved was really incompatible with the whole theology of the Vedas, and therefore with the supremacy of the Brahmins. Many of his chief disciples, many of the most distinguished members of his Order, were Brahmins."[1] It is more reasonable to suppose, and the supposition is borne out by His recorded sayings, that He met with no opposition just because He did *not* reject the soul theory with all that it involves; and when some of His followers committed this terrible blunder Buddhism

[1] *Op. cit.*, p. 115.

became extinct in India, for never will Hindus accept any so-called religion that casts aside belief in the Gods and in the immortality of man. As Dr. Rhys Davids says: "We should never forget that Gotama was born and brought up and lived and died a Hindu. His teaching, far-reaching and original as it was, and really subversive of the religion of the day, was Indian throughout. Without the intellectual work of his predecessors his own work, however original, would have been impossible.[1] He was no doubt the greatest of them all; and most probably the world will come to acknowledge him as, in many respects, the most intellectual of the religious teachers of mankind. But Buddhism is essentially an Indian system. The Buddha himself was, throughout his career, a characteristic Indian. And, whatever his position as compared with other teachers in the West, we need here only claim for him that he was the greatest and wisest and best of the Hindus."[2]

How continually He spake as Hindu to Hindus His similes and teachings often show, being drawn from the ancient Scriptures. Take as illustrations the threefold control of speech, mind, and body,[3] drawn from Manu; the sentence, "He who holds back rising anger like a rolling chariot, him I call a real driver; other people are but holding the reins," and the reference to the senses as well-broken horses, re-

[1] How then can we be asked to wrench the terms He uses away from all their previous connotations?

[2] *Op. cit.*, pp. 116, 117.

[3] *Dhammapada*, 281.

calling the teaching of Yama in the *Kathopanishad.*[1] The play on the higher and lower self,[2] from the *Bhagavad Gîtâ.* "All that we are is the result of what we have thought; it is founded on our thoughts, it is made up of our thought,"[3] from the *Chhândogyopanishad.* "It is good to control the mind, which is difficult to hold, unstable, and which goes where it pleases,"[4] a reminiscence of the *Bhagavad Gîtâ.* But it is useless to multiply instances. Enough that the Great Teacher carefully re-echoed the ancient writings, not as needing them Himself—He who knew all—but lest the ignorant should be caused to stumble and turn away from the faith of their fathers.

Let us now turn to the mass of teachings that confronts us, and learn from examples something not only of His precepts but of His methods. To a remarkable degree they were pointed, they were practical, and addressed to the consciences of his hearers. He never for one moment hesitated to speak in plainest language, in clearest terms, of the faults into which we are betrayed, of the mistakes into which men are constantly falling. For the Buddha was a Teacher indeed, a Teacher whose words illumined the mind. Strong and practical then, and for the most part it seems as if some passing incident gave the opportunity for a parable or a story, bearing an ethical lesson. His Bhikkhus were quarrelling, and as each man quarrelled with his

[1] *Ibid.*, 222, 94. [2] *Ibid.*, 380. [3] *Ibid.*, 1.
[4] *Udânavarga*, xxxi. 1.

neighbor, his neighbor returned the quarrel, and hatred ruled where peace ought to have been. Then the Buddha called them to Him, and He told them a story, the story of a king of Kâshî who made war against the king of Kosala, a small kingdom—and drove him away from his kingdom and took it to himself. The dispossessed king and his wife went and lived in a poor hovel, and there a son was born to them. The barber of the dispossessed king, seeing his former master, and desiring to curry the favor of the conqueror, betrayed to him the fugitive, and the king sent forth and seized the fugitive and his wife and gave them over to the executioner. As they were being led to the place of death, the son, who had been sent away for safety, came and saw his father and mother on their way to execution, and he pressed through the crowd. The father whispered, "My son be not long, be not short; hatred ceases not by hatred; by non-hatred it ceases;" and he then went on to death; and the son pondered over the father's words, he understood them not. Presently he took service under the king who had slain his mother and father after reducing them to beggary, and, attracting the king's attention, he was taken as his personal attendant. The king loved the youth and used to sleep with his head in his lap. As he slept there one day the young prince thought: "This king is in my power; he has slain my father and mother; he has reduced me to misery; he is helpless, I will slay him," and he drew out his sword. But his father's word came to his mind, "Be not short," and he knew it meant "Be not hasty in your action"; he put the sword back and remembered the other words, that hatred ceases not by hatred. The king awoke and said he dreamt that the prince he had dispossessed had slain him, and the youth, drawing his sword, revealed himself and told him that his life was at his mercy. The king prayed for his life, and the prince answered him: "Nay, O king, I have forfeited my life by this threat, and thou must give me back my life and thy pardon." So he gave the king his life that he could have taken, and the king pardoned the offence and gave him also his life, and then the prince told him of his father's dying words: "My father taught me that I must not be long—I must not keep hatred; I must not be short—I must not be hasty in action. That hatred ceases not by hatred at any time, but hatred ceases by love. For if I had slain thee, thy friends would have slain me in return, and my friends would then have slain thy friends, and so hatred would not have ceased; but now we have each given to the other his life, and thus hatred has ceased by love." Then the disciples became at one amongst themselves, and peace was restored within the Order.

The weeping mother, with dead babe clasped to bosom, is told her child shall be restored to her if she can bring some mustard-seed from a house where none has died; the gentle lesson sank more deeply than a hundred sermons.

A man abused Him vehemently as he was preaching the great doctrine: "A man who foolishly does me wrong, I will return to him the protection of my ungrudging love; the more evil comes from him, the more good shall go from me." While the man reproached Him, "Buddha was silent, and would not answer him, pitying his mad folly. The man having finished his abuse, Buddha asked him, saying: 'Son, when a man forgets the rules of politeness in making a present to another, the custom is to say, keep your present. Son! you have now railed at me; I decline to entertain your abuse, and request you to keep it, a source of misery to yourself. For as sound belongs to the drum, and shadow to the substance, so in the end misery will certainly overtake the evil-doer.' Buddha said: 'A wicked man who reproaches a virtuous one is like one who looks up and spits at Heaven; the spittle soils not the Heaven, but comes back and defiles his own person. So again, he is like one who flings dirt at another when the wind is contrary, the dirt does but return on him who threw it. The virtuous man cannot be hurt; the misery that the other would inflict comes back on himself.' "[1]

Sometimes a gleam of humor flashes out, and it is not difficult to picture the scene between the anxious disciple and the gentle, slightly amused, Master: "How are we to conduct ourselves, Lord, with regard to womankind?" "Don't see them, Ánanda." "But if we should see them what are we to do?"

[1] *The Sûtra of the Forty-two Sections*, translated by S. Beal from the Chinese. *Catena of Buddhist Scriptures*, pp. 193, 194.

"Abstain from speech, Ananda." "But if they should speak to us, Lord, what are we to do?" "Keep wide awake, Ananda."[1] Keep wide awake; notice what you are doing, guard your thoughts. A long sermon as to the wisdom of guarding himself from being led astray would not have been half as effective as that single sentence, "Keep wide awake, Ananda."

Among the striking characteristics of His teachings we find the occult fact that evil can only be put an end to by its opposite good: "Let a man overcome anger by love; let him overcome evil by good; let him overcome the greedy by liberality, the liar by truth."[2] A man must be strong and purposeful: "Earnestness is the path of immortality (Nirvana), thoughtlessness the path of death. Those who are in earnest do not die; those who are thoughtless are as if dead already."[3] Causation is unbroken: "If a man speaks or acts with an evil thought, pain follows him, as the wheel follows the foot of the ox that draws the carriage. . . . If a man speaks or acts with a pure thought, happiness follows him, like a shadow that never leaves him."[4] "He who has done even a little good finds in this world and in the other happiness and great profit; it is like seed that has well taken root. . . . He who has done what is evil cannot free himself of it; he may have done it long ago or afar off, he may have done it in solitude, but he cannot cast it off, and when it has ripened he can-

[1] *Maha-pari nibbana-Sutta*, 23. Sacred Books of the East, vol. xi. [2] *Dhammapada*, 223. [3] *Ibid.*, 21. [4] *Ibid.*, 1, 2.

not cast it off."[1] Above all, desire must be got rid of, as the root of all sorrow: "From desires comes grief, from desires comes fear; he who is free from desires knows neither grief nor fear. . . . It is hard for one who is held by the fetters of desire to free himself of them, says the Blessed One. The steadfast, who care not for the happiness of desires, cast them off and do soon depart. . . . As the shoemaker, when he has well prepared his leather, can use it to make shoes, so when one has cast off desires he has the highest happiness. . . . Desires are never satiated; wisdom affords contentment. . . . Not even in the pleasures of the Gods does the disciple of the perfect Buddha find pleasure; he rejoices only in the destruction of desires."[2] The teaching is pithily summed up: "Avoid doing all wicked actions, practise most perfect virtue, thoroughly subdue your mind, this is the doctrine of the Buddha."[3]

Most important is the teaching of the Buddha on "the subjugation of all the Asavas," of the outgoings of the life in man towards objects of desire. Of these there are seven classes, to be abandoned respectively by (1) insight—insight into the four noble truths, destroying the delusion of self, hesitation, and dependence on external rites; (2) by subjugation—the five senses and the mind; (3) by right use—clothes, alms, and abode, to be used, not delighted in; (4) by endurance—cold and heat, hunger and thirst, gadflies, mosquitoes, wind, sun, snakes,

[1] *Udanavarga*, xxviii. 25, 30.

[2] *Udanavarga*, ii. 2, 6, 12, 14, 18. [3] *Ibid.*, xxviii. i.

abusive words, bodily suffering, pains; (5) by avoidance—obvious dangers, improper places and companions; (6) by removal—evil thoughts; (7) by cultivation—the higher wisdom. When all this is done, "he has destroyed that craving Thirst, by thorough penetration of mind he has rolled away every Fetter, and he has made an end of Pain."[1]

His ethical teaching was pointed and direct to a rare degree; take for instance this: "The fault of others is easily perceived, but that of one's self is difficult to perceive; a man winnows his neighbor's faults like chaff, but his own fault he hides, as a cheat hides the bad die from the gambler. If a man looks after the faults of others, and is always inclined to be offended, his own passions will grow, and he is far from the destruction of passions."[2]

The Buddha was fond of forcing His questioners to answer their own questions. Instead of answering a question He questioned the questioner. Instead of laying down a doctrine or truth in answer to a question, He gradually led the man stage by stage to answer that question for himself—one of the wisest ways of teaching and the most likely of all ways to make a man realize the truth. Thus, when a young Brâhmana, by name Vâsettha, asked Him whether certain learned Brâhmanas showed the right way of reaching union with Brahmâ, the Buddha replied by a series of questions, the answers to

[1] *Sabbâsava-Sutta.* Sacred Books of the East, vol. xi.

[2] *Dhammapada*, 252, 253. Sacred Books of the East, vol. x.

which showed that the Brâhmanas neither knew Brahmâ nor were like Him, that while versed in the Vedas they were "omitting the practice of those qualities which really make a man a Brâhman, and adopting the practice of those qualities which really make men not Brâhmans," and at this point the Buddha summed up: "That these Brâhmans versed in the Vedas and yet bearing anger and malice in their hearts, sinful and uncontrolled, should after death, when the body is dissolved, become united to Brahmâ, who is free from anger and malice, sinless, and has self-mastery—such a condition of things has no existence." He then tells the youth that when the Tathâgata was asked the way that leads to the world of Brahmâ, He could give the answer: "For Brahmâ I know, Vâsettha, and the world of Brahmâ, and the path which leadeth unto it. Yea, I know it even as one who has entered the Brahmâ world, and has been born within it." "He, by Himself, thoroughly understands, and sees, as it were, face to face, this universe—the world below with all its spirits, and the worlds above, of Mâra and of Brahmâ—and all creatures, Samanas and Brâhmanas, Gods and men, and He then makes His knowledge known to others." When a man is attracted by the truth, and leaves his home, going forth into "the homeless state," and leading a noble and pure life, pervades the whole world "with heart of Love, far reaching, grown great and beyond measure," such a man is approaching union with Brahmâ; and that he "should after death, when the body is dissolved, become united with Brahmâ, who is the same—such a condition of things is every way possible."[1]

Here we have the key to all His teachings with regard to the Brâhmanas. Over and over again He says that they are to be treated with respect, that they are to be treated with reverence, but over and over again He also says that He does not call that man a Brâhmana who is vicious, who is uncontrolled, who is greedy, who is full of the vices of the world. So also He says as to His own Bhikkhus, that He does not call that man a Bhikkhu who wears a yellow robe and whose passions are uncontrolled. For the Buddha was not deceived by outward appearance, nor by the mere look of the outer man; He looked at the heart, and only when the heart was clean would He admit that the man had the right to bear a sacred name. He demanded, as every great teacher has demanded, that those who bear a sacred name should honor that name by the life they lead, and not bring scandal and discredit upon it by being full of passion and lust, anger and greed. His testimony to what they had been is full of interest. Asked by some Brâhmanas whether the Brâhmanas of His day were like the ancient Brâhmanas, He replied in the negative, and proceeded: "The old

[1] *Tevijja Sutta.* Sacred Books of the East, vol. xi. Here again we notice how the Buddha indorses the occult teachings as to the existence of the Gods, instead of pushing them aside, as the popular view often asserts. Of course, no one with knowledge could take up the modern materialistic idea now fathered on Buddhism.

sages were self-restrained, penitent; having abandoned the objects of the five senses, they studied their own welfare. There were no cattle for the Brâhmanas, nor gold, nor corn, (but) the riches and corn of meditation were for them, and they kept watch over the best treasure. . . Inviolable were the Brâhmanas, invincible, protected by the Dhamma, no one opposed them (while standing) at the doors of the houses anywhere. For forty-eight years they practised juvenile chastity; the Brâhmanas formerly went in search of science and exemplary conduct. The Brâhmanas did not marry (a woman belonging to) another (caste), nor did they buy a wife." They did not kill cows, "our best friends, in which medicines are produced," but sacrificed the gifts made to them. "They were graceful, large, handsome, renowned, Brâhmanas by nature, zealous for their different works; as long as they lived in the world, this race prospered. But there was a change in them." They began to covet wealth, they began to slay cows; "there were formerly three diseases: desire, hunger, and decay, but from the slaying of cattle there came ninety-eight." So things went from bad to worse, till, "Dhamma being lost, the Suddas and the Vessikas disagreed, the Khattiyas[1] disagreed in manifold ways, the wife despised her husband. The Khattiyas and the Brâhmanas and those others who had been protected by their castes, after doing away with their disputes on descent fell into the power of sen-

[1] Shûdras, Vaishyas, and Kshattryas.

sual pleasures."[1] How lofty was the opinion held by the Buddha of the true Brahmana may be read in the closing shlokas of the *Dhammapada*, in which, after giving the characteristics of the true Brâhmana, He concludes: "Him I call indeed a Brâhmana whose path the Gods do not know, nor spirits (Gandharvas), nor men, when passions are extinct, and who is an Arhat (venerable). Him I call indeed a Brâhmana who calls nothing his own, whether it be before, behind, or between, who is poor, and free from the love of the world. Him I call indeed a Brâhmana, the manly, the noble, the hero, the great sage, the conqueror, the impassible, the accomplished, the awakened. Him I call indeed a Brahmana who knows his former abodes, who sees heaven and hell, has reached the end of births, is perfect in knowledge, a sage, and whose perfections are all perfect."[2] The Buddha reaffirmed the ancient ideal, the essence of caste consisting in spiritual development, and if He declared that "a man does not become a Brâhmana by his platted hair, by his family, or by birth,"[3] he only declared what Manu had taught when the caste-system was ordained. Similarly He declared of His own monks: "A man is not a mendicant (Bhikkhu) simply because he asks others for alms; he who adopts the whole law is a Bhikkhu, not he who only begs. He who is above good and evil, who is chaste, who with knowledge passes through the world, he

[1] *Brahmanadhammikasutta*, in the *Sutta-nipâta*, trans. from the Pâli by V. Fausböll. Sacred Books of the East, vol. x., pt. ii. [2] *Dhammapada*, 420–423. [3] *Ibid.*, 393.

indeed is called a Bhikkhu." "Many men whose shoulders are covered with the yellow gown are ill-conditioned and unrestrained; such evil-doers by their evil deeds go to hell."[1] In the *Udânavarga*, the Tibetan recension of the *Dhammapada*, a chapter is devoted to the Brâhmana, and he is described as one who "is righteous, controlled, quiet, restrained, leading a life of holiness (brahmachârya), who neither harms nor kills any living thing." He "has reached the perfection (set forth in) the Vedas," he "is on the way to Nirvâna," he "has now a body for the last time," he "is tolerant with the intolerant," he "has crossed the stream."[2]

There is the ideal of the Brâhmana taught by the Buddha. There is the description of what the name should carry with it; and I appeal to the ancient Hindu Scriptures which indorse that contention. I appeal to such books as the Mahâbhârata, which contain exactly the same line of thought, and to the words of Manu, that the Brâhmana without the qualities of the Brâhmana was like "an elephant of wood and an antelope of leather"; the mere outward appearance of the thing, and not the reality. It is no more reasonable to speak of the Buddha as antagonistic to the Brâhmanas than to speak of Manu in exactly the same words, for both taught the same truth, that a man must have the inner life before he was worthy

[1] *Ibid.*, 266, 267, 307.

[2] *Op. cit.*, xxxiii. Trübner's Oriental Series, trans. from the Tibetan by W. W. Rockhill.

of the name. And if it be said, as I hear Hindus say, that he desired to abolish the Brâhmana caste because he thus pointed out the evil lives of Brâhmanas, then we shall have to argue that He wished to abolish His own order of Bhikkhus, because He declared that the yellow robe did not make the Bhikkhu, but that there must be self-restraint, true life, and the absence of worldly wealth. To represent the Buddha as an enemy of Brâhmanas and as seeking to destroy them as a caste, when all that He did was to hold up the ancient ideal and to reproach those whose lives dishonored it, is a perversion of facts. Had he succeeded in purifying the caste, He would thus have restored it to its ancient splendor; but He failed, alas! and its own poor ideals are hurrying it towards a self-chosen extinction. The occultist can but hold up the immortal ideal, and if men, rejecting it, perish, they perish.

Touching the Gods, the Buddha did not take the position often ascribed to Him, a position impossible to One who knew all worlds. He says that He Himself has visited all the worlds of the Gods, and therefore that He knows the way to them and is able to guide men along the path. And on one occasion when He was asked the way to the world of Brahmâ, He answered by asking the man whether he did not know the way to his own village, and whether he could not direct thither the wayfarer. The man answered that he was born there, and knew the way that led to it; so also, replied the Buddha, did He know the world of Brahmâ, having visited it and being familiar with it.[1]

We find frequent references to the Gods, indorsing the beliefs of the Hindus He addressed: "By earnestness did Maghavan[2] rise to the lordship of the Gods." "The disciple will overcome the earth, and the world of Yama, and the world of the Gods." "The Gods even envy him whose senses, like horses well broken in by the driver, have been subdued." (Note the simile taken from the *Kathopanishad.*) "Let us live happily then, though we call nothing our own. We shall be like the bright Gods, feeding on happiness." "Speak the truth; do not yield to anger; give, if thou art asked for little; by these three steps thou wilt go near the Gods."[3] In the southern Church the belief in the Gods appears to have disappeared, but man's ineradicable need to worship reappears in the adoration paid to the Buddha Himself. In the northern Church, less injured by materialism, the worship of the Gods survives, and they are worshipped under their Hindu names. There also we find the Trimûrti reappearing under Buddhist names: Shiva represented by Amitâbha, the Boundless Light; Vishnu by Padmapani, otherwise Avalokiteshvara; the Third being Mandjusri, "the representative of creative wisdom, corresponding to Brahma."[4]

Closely allied to the conception of the great hier-

[1] See *ante*, the answer to Vâsettha. [2] Indra.

[3] *Dhammapada*, 30, 43, 24, 167, 224.

[4] Sanskrit-Chinese Dictionary, Eitel, *sub voce*.

archies of Gods, are the ideas of "heaven" and "hell," regions of the world invisible through which man passes when out of the physical body—Devachan and part of Kâmaloka, the Theosophist calls them. The Buddha by no means ignored these states; in fact, we find Him describing both at length; many hells are mentioned in some detail by him in the *Mahâvagya*, in connection with the *post-mortem* fate of one of His Bhikkhus; again, in the *Mahâ-pari-nibbâna-sutta*, He declares of the wrong-doer: "On the dissolution of the body, after death, he is reborn into some unhappy state of suffering or woe," while the well-doer, under similar conditions, "is reborn into some happy state in heaven."[1] The northern Church Scriptures have very full accounts of the invisible worlds: there is the Kâma Loka, consisting of the earth and the four lower heavens, the abodes of Devas, Asuras, demons, beasts, and men (the physical and astral planes); then comes the abode of Mâra (astral) and the eighteen heavens of the Rûpa Loka (Rûpa Devachan or Svarga); and beyond these the Arûpa Loka of four heavens, "an ecstatic state of real existence; here dwell those disciples of Buddha who have not attained the imperishable nature." Beyond this is Nirvâna.[2] In regard to this, as with regard to some other of the more occult truths, the Scriptures of the northern Church seem to be fuller than those of the southern; the traditions

[1] *Op. cit.*, i. 23, 24.

[2] *Catena of Buddhist Scriptures*, summarized from Chinese Scriptures, pp. 89–91.

of the Arhats, to whom the Buddha gave in His old age the secret teachings, were carried into Tibet and China when the Buddhists fled away from India, and were there faithfully preserved.

His view of the small value of the so-called miraculous powers is recorded in the *Surangama Sûtra*,[1] where the Buddha is recorded to have said that by practising Samâdhi without any reliance on Bodhi—*i.e.*, seeking the Siddhis rather than Gnyâna[2]—men attained the power of flying through space, of invisibility, etc., and attained various degrees of sublime knowledge; but, not reaching wisdom, they were still bound to the wheel of transmigration.

Much controversy has arisen over the apparent denial, by the southern Church, of a continuing Ego, passing from life to life. Such Orientalists as Dr. Rhys Davids insist on it, and much of the popular Hindu distrust of Buddhism arises from the general belief that they do not believe in the Ego. The teachings of the Buddha Himself, however, are clear enough. Thus, when asked about some of His disciples who had died, "Where has he been reborn and what is his destiny?" He answered that one had reached emancipation; another "has become a Sakadâgâmin, who on his first return to this world will make an end of sorrow;" another was "no longer liable to be reborn in a state of suffering;" in all these cases, a persisting individuality is obviously taken for granted. A disciple may say of himself: "Hell is destroyed for me; and rebirth as an animal,

[1] *Ibid.*, pp. 30, 31. [2] Seeking powers rather than wisdom.

or a ghost, or in any place of woe. I am converted; I am no longer liable to be reborn in a state of suffering, and am assured of final salvation."[1] So also He said that those who died while "they with believing heart are journeying on such pilgrimage shall be reborn, after death, when the body is dissolved, in the happy realms of heaven."[2] The doctrine of the Self from the Vinâya has already been quoted. And we find Him saying, like any other Hindu: "For Self is the lord of self; Self is the refuge of self,"[3] a sentence meaningless if there be no Self.

In fact the whole teaching loses its reasonableness and falls into ruins if the fundamental teaching be withdrawn of an Ego that passes from birth to birth in the cycle of reincarnation and merges in the Self when emancipation is gained. This is the Hindu teaching, and the Buddha built His teachings on its universal acceptance among His hearers. In the northern Church the doctrine remained unchallenged of the "true man without a position"; the Lin-tsi School teach: "Within the body which admits sensations, acquires knowledge, thinks, and acts, [compare the statement regarding the Self in the Vinâya] there is the 'true man without a position,' Wu-wei-chenjen. He makes himself clearly visible; not the thinnest separating film hides him. Why do you

[1] *Mahâ-parinibbâna-sutta*, ii. 6–10.

[2] *Ibid.*, v. 22. The pilgrimage is to any one of the four places at which the Buddha was respectively born, reached illumination, founded the kingdom of truth, and died.

[3] *Dhammapada*, 380.

not recognize him? The invisible power of the mind permeates every part. . . . This is Buddha, the Buddha within you."[1]

Next should be considered His teaching of "the Path," which depends entirely upon the continuity of life. The Path, in Buddhism, has the same stages as those given by Shri Shankarâchârya, both as to the preliminary Path and the Path itself. The Buddha asks from His disciples as the first qualification that opening of the mind which is identical with discrimination or Viveka, discrimination between the permanent and the impermanent; the second step is that regarding action, which teaches indifference to the fruits of action and is identical with Vairâgya; then follow the six qualities of the mind, the same six recounted the day before yesterday in speaking of the same Path as taught in Hinduism; fourthly, the deep longing for liberation, the same as Mumuksha; and lastly, the gotrabhû, the same as the adhikari, when the man is ready for Initiation. After Initiation comes the Path itself, traced in the following quotation, which begins at the highest stage and follows it backward: "Buddha said: The Rahat [Arhat] is able to fly through the air, change his appearance, fix the years of his life, shake heaven and earth. The successive stages towards this condition of being are: The Anâgâmin, who, at the expiration of his life (years) ascends in a spiritual form to the nineteen heavens, and in one of these completes his destiny, by becoming a Rahat. Next is the condi-

[1] *Chinese Buddhism*, pp. 163, 164.

tion of a Sakrâdâgâmin, in which, after one birth and death, a man becomes a Rahat. Next, the condition of Srotâpânna, in which, after seven births and deaths, a man becomes a Rahat. These are they who, having entirely separated themselves from all desire and lust, are like branches of a tree, cut off and dead."[1]

Thus the Buddha taught His disciples, as the Scriptures still record, and we have the right to use these Scriptures against the misconceptions of those who, materialized in their own thought, are impatient of the verities of the world invisible.

Arhatship was the last step ere attaining complete liberation and gaining the Nirvânic consciousness. The teaching of the Buddha as to Nirvâna is, perhaps, the clearest on record, being positive instead of, as is usual, negative. Having said that the Bhikkhu should concentrate within himself all his mental faculties, "as the tortoise draws its body into his shell," the Lord proceeds to tell of Nirvâna: "Bhixus, the uncreated, the invisible, the unmade, the elementary, the unproduced, exist (as well as) the created, the visible, the made, the conceivable, the compound, the produced; and there is an uninterrupted connection between the two. Bhixus, if the uncreated, the invisible, the unmade, the elementary, the unproduced, was nonentity, I could not say that the result of their connection from cause to effect with the created, the visible, the made, the compound, the conceivable, was final emancipation.

[1] *Sûtra of the Forty-two Sections. Chinese Buddhism*, 191.

. . . The impermanency of the created, the visible, the made, the produced, the compound, the great torment of subjection to old age, death, and ignorance, what proceeds from the cause of eating; (all this) is destroyed, and there is found no delight in it; this is the essential feature of final emancipation. Then there will be no doubts and scruples; all sources of suffering will be stopped, and one will have the happiness of the peace of the sanskâra. . . . This is the chief (beatitude) of those who have reached the end, perfect and unsurpassable peace, the destruction of all characteristics, the perfection of perfect purity, the annihilation of death."[1] Such is his description of a state in which He ever dwelt, whether in or out of the body; yet we find people who instead of believing in the annihilation of death, believe in the annihilation of life in Nirvâna. I know no Scripture in which the truth as to Nirvâna is put as plainly as it is here. It is existence, and not non-existence; it is reality and not non-reality; it is permanency, and not transitoriness. What is meant by "Nirvâna," by the "going out" implied in the name, is, He declares, the going out of all these impermanent things; these disappear and then man attains his final emancipation.

For forty-five years did the Lord Buddha wander over Northern India, teaching, until His work was done and He came to the laying aside of His body. A strange story is attached to His outgoing, significant enough in the old days, but read in a literal sense

[1] *Udanavarga*, xxvi. 1, 21, 22, 24, 31.

in these modern days, by those who eat pigs. Chunda, a worker in metals, shortly after the Buddha had announced His approaching departure, offered Him His daily meal and prepared dried boar's flesh, sweet rice, and cakes. The Lord bade Chunda serve Him only with the boar's flesh, giving the rice and cakes to the disciples, and bade him bury what of the boar's flesh remained; for "I see no one, Chunda, on earth nor in Mâra's heaven, nor in Brahmâ's heaven, no one among Samanas and Brâhmanas, among Gods and men, by whom, when he has eaten it, that food can be assimilated, save by the Tathâgata."[1] Surely such words are enough to show that the "boar's flesh" was not physical food, such as men who live on flesh assimilate without difficulty. After eating, He taught, and then sickness fell on Him and great pain; He bore it calmly, and recovering went on His way. That same day His skin was observed to shine with exceeding splendor, and He told Ánanda that it was the sign of his departing that night, and lying down He rested for a while, and arising went to the Sâla grove of the Mallas, and lay between the twin Sâla trees, with His head to the north; the trees showered on Him their flowers, and heavenly flowers fell and heavenly music sounded, in homage to the dying Lord, but He spake to Ánanda and said that while such homage was due to Him, yet worthier was the homage paid by the pure and noble man or woman who obeyed His law. All the Devas of the worlds gathered, and crowds of

[1] *Maha-parinibbana-sutta*, 19.

men came to pay their last homage, and the Buddha made His last Arhat, the mendicant Sabhadda; five hundred disciples stood round Him at the ending, and he spake His last words: "Behold, now, brethren, I exhort you," saying, "Decay is inherent in all component things. Work out your salvation with diligence." Then silence fell, and He passed into deepest meditation, and returned not.

As a king of kings, His body was prepared for the burning, and was laid on a pyre of all fragrant woods; it left no ash, but the bones remained. These were divided as sacred relics, and carried away in eight portions, each to be placed under a Thûpa, and a ninth Thûpa was erected over the vessel in which His body had been burned, and a tenth, by the Moriyas, over the embers of His funeral pile. So ended the noblest life yet lived by one of our humanity, of the first who on this globe has attained Buddhahood. "Bow down with clasped hands! Hard, hard is a Buddha to meet with through hundreds of ages!"[1]

There is no time to trace the later growth of Buddhism, the development of its different schools of philosophy, the arising of noble teachers trained in its wisdom, the materializing of the faith that followed its introduction among less developed and less metaphysically inclined people, and its maintenance

[1] The closing words of the *Mahâ-parinibbâna-sutta*, from which the above account of his departure is summarized, any passages in inverted commas being textual quotations.

in its original purity in its esoteric schools. Enough has been said of the sayings of the Buddha Himself to substantiate my position as to the identity of the teachings and the training in Hinduism and Buddhism, and to justify my plea for love and amity between the two faiths that belong to the Hindu people and are the glory of the Hindu race. This teaching of the Buddha, of the Mighty, of the Enlightened One, who first of all in our humanity climbed the ladder of Buddhahood, is the ancient teaching reproclaimed. There are hatred and division too often between Hinduism and Buddhism; there are suspicion and doubt and antagonism, which have made a great gulf between the two mighty religions, and men will not try to bridge it either on the one side or on the other. Yet the Teachers of both belong to the same Brotherhood; the disciples of both are going towards the same Brotherhood; there is no difference there between the Hindu Master and the Buddhist Master, for both teach the same essential verities, and have come along the path common to both religions. Born on Indian soil, speaking with Indian lips, reproducing the noblest moralities of the Hindu Scriptures, recognizing the Hindu Gods, the Buddha is still rejected by the Indian people as a Teacher though inconsistently worshipped as an Avatâra by many of the orthodox Hindus. Why should there be enmity instead of brotherhood, why should there be suspicion and hatred instead of peace? This mighty religion that moulds so many million minds, this noble philosophy that trains so many million intellects, this life—the most perfect in its details of which there is any record amongst the histories of men, evolved in our race—why should you exclude them from your sympathy, why withhold from them your reverence and your love? The Buddha comes to you a man of your own race, the glory of the Hindu nation, born in the Kshatriya caste, belonging to the Âryan people, teaching the ancient truths in a new form, and making them ready for the training of vaster multitudes. He is ours, as He is also the world's; greatest among its teachers, purest and fairest of all the blossoms of humanity, this flower flowered on the Indian soil, this teacher spake the Indian tongue, and loved the Indian people. He taught them, He worked for them, He healed them, He instructed them; and then His compassion flowed outward, overflowed the worlds. Then surely we may reverence Him, the Blessed One, the Lord, the Teacher. He is admitted to be Teacher among the Gods; he may well also be done homage to as Teacher among men.

Hinduism and Buddhism would do well if—mother and daughter—they rushed together again in a motherly and filial embrace, and forgot in that embrace the history of their estrangement, forgot in that embrace the history of their long separation. Then would the Indian home again be at one, one rooftree covering mother and daughter alike, thus able to influence the Western world with one lip and with one tongue, helping forward the redemption of that humanity of which the Buddha was born and for which He lived. Let all re-echo the words which close the account of His departure: "Bow down with clasped hands! Hard, hard is a Buddha to meet with through hundreds of ages!"

CHRISTIANITY.

Brothers, in dealing this morning with the subject of Christianity there are certain special difficulties which we did not have to face in speaking of the other three great religions with which we have been dealing on the last three mornings. These special difficulties arise from certain distinct causes. First, there is a certain historical obscurity affecting its origin, due to the struggles through which it passed in its early days, in a time when records were not carefully kept, and when an enormous mass of spurious documents under sacred names were put forward, at first blindly accepted, and then gradually sifted out. The obscurity would not matter, as it can be quickly dissipated by the light of occult knowledge; but if this be done, many present-day Christians would feel bitterly aggrieved, as though the essentials of their faith were being attacked. Our next great difficulty is the immense difference—or rather the immense differences—that separate the Christians amongst themselves, so that, whatever line one may take, one is likely to have some of the Christians saying that Christianity has been misrepresented, inasmuch as it has not been taken along their special line. For we have the Greek Church and the Roman Catholic Church, embracing a vast majority of the

Christian population; then we have a very large number of different churches and sects classed together under the title of "Protestants"—an awkward name to deal with, because it affirms nothing, but simply declares its protest against opinions held by other Christians. Hence in these three divisions, as I will call them for the moment, we find a great number of serious contradictions, and the student who desires to give a fair exposition and in no sense to misrepresent finds himself in a whirlpool of conflicting statements, the acceptation of any one of which brings him into conflict with others. There is nothing, outside the Bible and the Apostle's Creed, that by the whole of the Christian world would be taken as a fair representation of Christian doctrine, and disputes as to the meaning of these abound. The extraordinary importance attached by all sections of the Christian world to the form of intellectual belief causes a bitterness of controversy unknown to other creeds, accuracy of belief being a far more stringent condition of membership in most of the churches than submission to any rule of conduct.

I propose to do here as I have done in dealing with the other religions—to take the Scriptures, the accepted Scriptures, of the whole religion and base my exposition upon them; I shall further use the documents of the early Church, the teachings of the "Fathers of the Church," as they are called, as elucidating the Scriptures; and then, using the light of occultism, I shall try to disentangle what is essential from the non-essential, to disentangle that which is real and true from the accretions which have grown over it by lack of knowledge and very often by the exigencies of controversies. One other great difficulty remains, and this is one which deals with the emotions rather than with the intellect. Christianity alone among the religions of the world claims to be unique; every other religion claims authority over its own adherents, and stands as it were on its own ground, admitting the value of other religions and holding towards them, as a rule, a position of benevolent neutrality, not of active opposition. But with regard to Christianity, this is not the case. Christianity claims to be the one revelation, the unique voice of God to man. It permits no rivals on its platform; it admits no brothers into its household; it claims to stand by itself, alone, unapproachable, classing together all the other religions of the world as mistaken, sometimes under the contemptuous name of Heathen, sometimes rather more courteously but still in the same exclusive spirit. This, of course, stirs up angry feelings both on the one side and the other. The Christian propagandist insists on the supreme value of his own faith, and the small value of others; while on the other hand the members of other faiths, resenting the assumption of superiority, feel moved to an opposition towards Christianity which they do not feel as regards the non-missionary faiths of the world. Especially in a country like this, those who do not belong to the Christian religion see what I cannot but call its worst side, its side of antagonism, very often accompanied, unfortunately, by insult and outrage as regards the elder religions; so that it is very difficult to gain your sympathetic understanding of what the religion really is in itself, for you have seen it under the most unfavorable aspect, on its militant rather than on its really religious side. I shall then have to ask you this morning to drop out of your minds, for the time, everything that has outraged your religious feelings, everything that may have roused in you emotions of antagonism, and to look on this religion as you more easily look upon others, as a way in which the Supreme is training a large number of His human family, as a religion that brings help and comfort and spiritual teaching to millions of the human race. If it suffers, as it often does, by the unwisdom of its militant representatives, try to forget that, and to look at the religion as a religion and not as a proselytizing agency.

Let us, with this preface—which in this country is a necessary introduction, if I am to win any sympathy at all for this, which is one of the great religions of the world—let us look at the authorities, and see what we have to deal with in the study of the religion, how far we can understand the environment in which it gradually grew up, for without a study of that environment you will never understand the latter presentation of the doctrines, you will never be able to realize the fashion in which it grew.

First of all, we have certain "canonical books" accepted equally by all divisions of Christendom, as to which there arises no challenge at all from Greek,

Roman Catholic, or Protestant churches. They all alike accept without questioning certain books, which are classed together under the names of the *Old* and *New Testaments*, together forming the *Bible*, as books which contain the divine revelation, anything contrary to which is regarded as heretical. The *Old Testament*, the more ancient division of these canonical Scriptures, consists of a large number of different books, many of them historical, received from the Jewish or the Hebrew nation. Their writing extended over a long period of time, and the succession of books is marked by a very distinct growth from a comparatively barbarous condition—wherein the religion was narrow, filled with sacrifices of a peculiarly bloodthirsty character—down to the later times when the Hebrew people, having largely come into touch with other civilizations, especially with those dominated by the religion of Zoroaster, took into their own faith a nobler, a grander conception of the divine Being, which you find expounded in the prophetic books; these contain some most noble passages as regards the nature of God, and also as regards the righteousness which God demands from men. I shall refer presently to these more in detail, but will first finish the question of authorities. In the *Old Testament* we have further the *Psalms*, which are songs somewhat of the nature of the songs that we find in other religions, like those that are in the Vedas, like the Gathas of the Zoroastrians; some of them marked by the most elevated and noble spirit, some of them belonging to the earlier stage, exceedingly militant in their character, and by no means always very good or high in their morality. We then come to the documents included under the title the *New Testament*. This consists of four Gospels, containing the life of the Founder of the religion, an account of the early Church, a number of epistles written by His followers to the different sections of the infant Church, and a book of prophecies. There is comparatively little doctrine in the gospels themselves; certain doctrines may be deduced from them, but there is little authoritative statement; rather do you find a large number of ethical precepts, a large number of the teachings of the Christ, more of an ethical than of a philosophical character; then in the epistles are contained most of the dogmatic statements giving the outline of the doctrines of the faith. Outside this canon, selected from a mass of documents, so far as the *New Testament* is concerned, we have what are called apocryphal Scriptures. The apocryphal Scriptures of the Jews are distinctly remarkable works, one of them especially, *the Book of Wisdom*, being a document of rare beauty and showing great spirituality. These are more thoroughly accepted by the Roman Catholics than they are by the Protestant Churches. In the Roman Catholic *Bibles* they are generally bound between the *Old* and *New Testaments*, whereas in the majority of Protestant *Bibles* they are dropped out as non-canonical. Next we have a mass of apocrypha in connection with the early Church, the gospels of Mary, of Peter, of James, and so on—stories of the Infancy of Jesus, stories of His later life, stories of His descent into hell, of His work in the invisible world—a mass of writings, very many of them exceedingly interesting, as showing the literature of primitive Christianity, interesting and instructive for the student, and necessary to be studied, if he would know what I may call the intellectual environment of the early Church. These are never bound up with the book called the *Bible;* they form a great mass of literature, a very large number of documents, which a student ought to read if he desires to understand early Christianity at all. Lastly, we have an immense literature, that of the fathers, of the bishops, of the teachers, of the early Church, running especially over the latter part of the second through the third, fourth, and fifth centuries—once more a mass of voluminous literature, without a knowledge of which no one is competent to pass an opinion upon Christian doctrine, nor to stand up as a teacher or an exponent of Christianity. This literature was written by most learned men, men of whom many have been sainted by the later Church, like S. Clement of Alexandria, S. Irenæus, and many others. These are documents of enormous value in understanding the growth of Christianity, and it is very largely due to the utter carelessness of the Protestant churches regarding them, and the dense ignorance of their contents which as a rule you find among the less-instructed Protestant clergy, that Christianity is often presented in so crude, so narrow, and so unphilosophical an aspect, that many of the educated reject it because it seems to them to be irrational. If the Protestant churches studied this literature, as Roman Catholics most certainly do, they would have much more hold than they have to-day on the cultured intellect of Europe, for you have in these documents the philosophic, the metaphysical basis of Christianity. Yet, if you go outside the Church of England, where do you find many learned Protestant clergy thoroughly conversant with these documents? If you go into the dissenting churches, you very rarely come across a minister who has studied them in any fashion, and so you get that peculiar class who echo the statement that the "*Bible*, and the *Bible* alone, is the religion of Protestants." The result of this is a most unphilosophical form of Christianity, unfairly discrediting it in the minds of the thinking, the intellectual, and the philosophic few. With regard to the oral traditions—for they are largely oral traditions that you find in the four Gospels that contain the life of the Founder—these were selected rather late in the second century, and were put together under the names of four of the great apostles of the Church. That they were selected from many other documents is clear from the preamble to the third Gospel, in which the writer begins by saying: "Forasmuch as many have taken in hand to set forth in order a declaration of those things which are most surely believed amongst us, even as they delivered them unto us, which from the beginning were eye-witnesses and ministers of the word; it seemed good to me also, having a perfect understanding of all things from the very first, to write unto thee in order," and so he also writes his gospel. Now that is an important point as showing you the way in which these accounts were written. First, from mouth to mouth the story spread. In Christianity, as in other religions, there was an immense mass of oral tradition handed from mouth to mouth and uncommitted to writing. Many of the sacred teachings were never written down at all, as we shall find from the testimony of some of the fathers of the Church; the creed which every Christian was taught to recite was not written, but was only taught by word of mouth to be used as a sign of recognition of a certain status in the Church. That period of oral teaching is of considerable importance, and its existence is further proved by the quotations of the sayings of Jesus given in the earliest fathers, by men like Justin Martyr, Ignatius, the Shepherd of Hermas, and others, who quote as the sayings of the Lord sentences which are not to be found in the canonical gospels at all, but which are found in the so-called apocrypha. The canonical are selections from a larger tradition, put together at a later date. We shall have to glance at Clement of Alexandria, one of the greatest fathers of the Church, at Tertullian, at Origen, who have left voluminous writings, helping us to see in detail the condition of the Church in their times; and these we shall rely upon to establish certain fundamental positions, without which you will do injustice to Christianity, as so many of its own adherents do it injustice to day.

First among these preliminary positions comes the division of Christian teaching into two parts—the revealed and the unrevealed, the exoteric and the esoteric doctrines. This division existed among the Hebrews who so much influenced the earlier tradition of Christianity, and who had the secret system known under the name of the Kabalah. I am not going to speak upon it now, although that also should be known by the earnest student of Christianity. But I want to draw your attention to certain statements of the Christ to His apostles, and of the earlier teachers, which prove beyond the possibility of challenge the existence of hidden or esoteric teaching, the loss of which in some parts of the Church explains very largely the crude statement that we now hear made as to God and as to the human soul. First of all let us take one or two statements of the Christ Himself as regards the fashion of His own teaching. There comes in the forefront of it His declaration to His apostles: "Unto you it is given to know the mystery of the kingdom of God, but unto them that are without all those things are done in parables."[1] Origen commented on this declaration of the Christ as follows: "I have not yet spoken of the observance of all that is written in the Gospels, each one of which contains much doctrine difficult to be understood, not merely by the multi-

[1] *S. Mark*, iv. 11.

tude, but even by certain of the more intelligent, including a very profound explanation of the parables which Jesus delivered to 'those without,' while reserving the exhibition of their full meaning for those who had passed beyond the stage of exoteric teaching, and who came to him privately in the house. And when he comes to understand it, he will admire thereas on why some are said to be 'without' and others 'in the house.'"[1] Thus Origen draws a distinction between those that are without, the unlettered, the unlearned multitude, who could only be taught the elements of truth by way of parables, and those who were within the house, apostles and disciples, to whom the word of God was revealed in its entirety, the mysteries of the kingdom which were not given at all to the outer world. Then again we find Jesus saying to His disciples words that admit of no misconception: "Give not that which is holy unto the dogs, neither cast ye your pearls before swine, lest they trample them under their feet."[2] The meaning of the words "dogs" is known to us not only from its use by Jewish historians, but from the lips of Jesus Himself. The word was used to describe every nation that was not of the seed of Abraham. And we find that when a Syro-Phœnician woman came to Jesus and asked Him to exercise his miraculous power, His first answer was: "It is not meet to

[1] *Contra Celsum*, XXI. Not having the Fathers at hand, I have availed myself for the quotations from them of Mr. A. M. Glass' excellent series of articles in *Lucifer*, on "Christianity and its Teachings."

[2] *S. Matthew*, vii. 6.

take the children's bread and to cast it to dogs." She meekly accepted the title and replied; "Yet the dogs eat of the crumbs which fall from their master's table."[1] So that the meaning of the word "dog" is by no means in dispute; it means those who are not within the limits of the kingdom of God. So the early fathers understood the meaning and obeyed it. They used exactly the same policy. Clement of Alexandria, quoting these very words, says that it is difficult to teach "swinish and untrained hearers."[2] So again Jesus says to His disciples: "I have yet many things to say unto you, but ye cannot bear them now."[3] According to the traditions of the fathers He remained on earth after His resurrection for eleven years, teaching His apostles the secret things. S. Clement says of this sacred knowledge: "It was spoken from the beginning to those only who understood. Now that the Saviour has taught the Apostles, the unwritten rendering of the written [Scriptures] has been handed down also to us."[4] According to the *Acts* he only remained for forty days, but during these forty days He instructed them as to the things of the kingdom of God,[5] and those instructions remained unrecorded. There is no trace of them in the canonical Scriptures of the Church. In fact, Origen observes on this very fact that Jesus "conversed with His disciples in private, and especially in their secret retreats, concerning the gospel of God; but the words which He uttered

[1] *S. Matthew*, xv. 26, 27. [2] *Stromata*, I. xii.
[3] *S. John*, xvi. 12. [4] *Stromata*, VI. xv. [5] *Acts*, i. 3.

have not been preserved."[1] Just in the same way do we find Saint Paul speaking. He tells his converts of the Church of Corinth: "I, brethren, could not speak unto you as unto spiritual, but as unto carnal, even as unto babes in Christ."[2] Again: "We speak the wisdom of God in a mystery, even the hidden wisdom,"[3] and "we speak wisdom amongst them that are perfect;"[4] not amongst the generality but amongst the perfect, a name which is well recognized in its technical meaning—from the statements in the fathers—those who have been initiated into the mysteries and are therefore the perfected within the Church. I might quote other texts, but these may suffice, and we will turn to the practice of the Church, as shown in the fathers. Clement of Alexandria states that in his writings he only intended to recall to his readers truth they had received more fully in oral exposition: "The writing of these memoranda of mine, I well know, is weak, when compared with that spirit, full of grace, which I was privileged to hear. But it will be an image to recall the archetype to him who was struck with the Thyrsus,"[5] a phrase every occultist will understand. "It is not to be wished," he writes, "that all things should be exposed indiscriminately to all and sundry, or the benefits of wisdom communicated to those who have not, even in a dream, been purified in soul (for it is not allowed to hand to every chance comer what has been procured with such laborious efforts); nor

[1] *Contra Celsum*, VI. vi. [2] 1 *Corinthians*, iii. 1.
[3] *Ibid.*, ii. 7. [4] *Ibid.*, ii. 6. [5] *Stromata*, I., i.

are the mysteries of the word to be expounded to the profane."[1] When Celsus assailed Christianity as a secret system, Origen answered: "To speak of the Christian doctrine as a *secret* system is altogether absurd. Bnt that there should be certain doctrines, not made known to the multitude, which are [revealed] after the exoteric ones have been taught, is not a peculiarity of Christianity alone, but also of philosophic systems, in which certain truths are exoteric and others esoteric."[2] In order to preserve due order, Christian converts were led successively through different stages; at first they were hearers, then catechumens, and then, receiving baptism, they became full members of the Church. Within the Church itself were also grades: first came the general members; out of these, the pure in life went on into a second grade: "Whoever is pure, not only from all defilement, but from what are regarded as lesser transgressions, let him be boldly initiated in the mysteries of Jesus, which properly are made known only to the holy and the pure. . . . He who acts as initiator, according to the precepts of Jesus, will say to those who have been purified in heart: 'He whose soul has, for a long time, been conscious of no evil, and especially since he yielded himself to the healing of the word, let such a one hear the doctrines which were spoken in private by Jesus to his genuine disciples.'"[3] These were the "few chosen" out of the many who were "called," and beyond

[1] *Stromata*, V. ix.

[2] *Contra Celsum*, I. vii.

[3] *Ibid.*, III. lx.

these were still "the chosen of the chosen," with "perfect knowledge," and who "lived in perfection of righteousness according to the gospel."[1] Tertullian complains of the heretics that they did not preserve this order, but treated every one equally: "To begin with, it is doubtful who is a catechumen and who is a believer; they have all access alike, they hear alike, they pray alike—even heathens, if any such happen to come among them. 'That which is holy they will cast to the dogs, and their pearls,' although (to be sure) they are not real ones, 'they will fling to the swine.'"[2]

Part of this teaching, at least, concerned the true meaning of the Scriptures, which were by no means accepted as mere historical and ethical documents as they are to-day. Origen explains—and his statements are especially valuable, since he is stated by Socrates to have been an "expositor of the mystical tradition of the Church"[3]—that Scripture is threefold in meaning: the "flesh" for simple men; the "soul" for the more instructed; the spirit for the "perfect," and he quotes the already mentioned words of St. Paul as to the "wisdom of God in a mystery." The histories are the "flesh," and are very useful to the simple and ignorant, but often absurdities are introduced in order to show that there is a hidden meaning, and the gospels "do not contain throughout a pure history of events, which are interwoven indeed according to the letter, but which did not actually

[1] *Stromata.* [2] *De Præscriptione Hæreticorum*, xli.
[3] *Ecclesiastical History*, III. v.

occur." "The gospels themselves are filled with the same kind of narratives; *e.g.*, the devil leading Jesus up into a high mountain . . . and the attentive reader may notice in the gospels innumerable other passages like these, so that he will be convinced that in the histories that are literally recorded circumstances that did not occur are inserted."[1] Some hints are given by various fathers as to their methods of scriptural interpretation, and it is evident that a very complete system existed, one of the keys, at least, being numerical. But we have not time to follow this attractive byway. Enough for our purpose to show that Christianity, like other great religions, had its secret teaching, confined to the few. This was lost, for the most part, in the flood of ignorance which swept over Europe after the fall of the Roman Empire, and the crude interpretation, the teaching for the multitude, replaced the spiritual truths known to the few. A few fragments survived, in the custody of the Greek and Latin churches, and symbols and ceremonies still tell of their original presence, but as a systematic teaching they disappear, leaving Christianity shorn of its strength. Too often now teaching is condemned by Protestants unless it is teaching which the most ignorant, the most unlearned, the most childish, can understand; and the result of this policy in Protestant countries is that while the churches keep hold of the ignorant, they lose their hold upon the more learned; for the presentation of God and of nature

[1] *De Principiis*, IV. i.

that satisfies the mind of the child, that satisfies the mind of men utterly unphilosophical and uncultured, must ever be a representation that repels the mind of the philosopher, whose wider and deeper faculties demand something more than that which satisfies the dawning faculties of the other. In this way Christianity has become weakened, in this way scepticism has largely developed, and we find men throwing aside the whole of Christianity, because the presentment made to them is utterly unworthy of intellectual apprehension, and because it contradicts the plainest facts of science.

Let us now hastily trace the religious evolution of the Hebrew nation, in order that we may understand the place in it of the Founder of Christianity, the conception of God current in His time, and also the changes through which that conception had passed. In the earliest books of the Hebrew Scriptures we have a very limited conception of God, and however true they may be as regards the lower Gods, comparatively narrow in their individuality, and limited in their power as all the lower Gods must necessarily be, some of the ideas are utterly revolting when they are applied to the Supreme Deity, and are given as descriptions of the one God, the Supreme LOGOS, He who presides over the universe, the Life and Supporter of all. I need only remind you in passing, of many statements, such as the way in which this limited representative of the divine came down to walk in the garden of Eden, came down to upset the builders of the tower of Babel, and so on, for you to realize at once that you are face to face with the lower divine entities and not with the Logos. But let us pass on from those, with all the bloody sacrifices that surrounded them, and take the nobler conception of the prophets, which moulded the later views adopted in the Christian Church. Here you find an idea of God which is lofty and pure in character. He is essentially holy, the Holy One of Israel; He is "the high and lofty One that inhabiteth eternity, whose name is holy";[1] He is "God the Lord, He that created the heavens and stretched them out, He that spread forth the earth, and that which cometh out of it; He that giveth breath unto the people upon it, and spirit to them that walk therein."[2] He is the one, the only God: "Before me there was no God formed, neither shall there be after me. I, even I, am the Lord; and beside me there is no saviour."[3] In connection with this nobler view of God we can see many traces of the influence upon the Hebrew captives of the Zoroastrian belief. Their ideas before and after the captivity are entirely different. There is also a demand for righteousness, for purity, a contempt for outward observances when they were not connected with inner nobility of character, a contempt which is sometimes even fierce in its expression, as though there were overmastering indignation at the idea that any would dare to offer to a holy God the mere outer ceremonies, instead of a righteous and noble life. Take for instance that very strong passage that you

[1] *Isaiah*, lvii. 15. [2] *Ibid.*, xlii. 5. [3] *Ibid.*, xliii. 10, 11.

find in the prophet Amos: "I hate, I despise your feast-days, and I will not smell in your solemn assemblies. Though ye offer me burnt offerings and your meat offerings, I will not accept them, neither will I regard the peace offerings of your fat beasts. Take thou away from me the noise of thy songs; for I will not hear the melody of thy viols. But let judgment run down as waters, and righteousness as a mighty stream."[1] That is the spirit of the later prophets. You may take another example from Isaiah, where the people are complaining that though they fast God has not listened to them, that they have afflicted their bodies and their souls and He takes no notice; and then the answer comes thundering as from Sinai· "Ye shall not fast as ye do this day, to make your voice to be heard on high. Is it such a fast that I have chosen? a day for a man to afflict his soul? is it to bow down his head as a bulrush, and to spread sackcloth and ashes under him? wilt thou call this a fast, and an acceptable day to the Lord? Is not this the fast that I have chosen: to loose the hands of wickedness, to undo the heavy burdens, and to let the oppressed go free, and that ye break every yoke? Is it not to deal thy bread to the hungry, and that thou bring the poor that are cast out to thy house? when thou seest the naked that thou cover him; and that thou hide not thyself from thine own flesh? Then shall thy light break forth as the morning, and thine health shall spring forth speedily; and thy righteousness shall go before

[1] *Amos*, v. 21–24.

thee; the glory of the Lord shall be thy rereward. There is the moral side coming out as it comes out over and over again in these prophets. Only one other quotation will I give you, to show the mental environment, as it were, in which Jesus was born, and that is a word from the prophet Micah, which sums up human duty. The prophet asks himself how he shall please God and what he shall do: "Wherewith shall I come before the Lord, and bow myself before the high God? shall I come before Him with burnt offerings, with calves of a year old? Will the Lord be pleased with thousands of rams, or with ten thousands of rivers of oil? shall I give my first-born for my transgression, the fruit of my body for the sin of my soul? He hath showed thee, O man, what is good; and what doth the Lord require of thee, but to do justly, and to love mercy, and to walk humbly with thy God?"[2] That is the strong and sound morality that you find coming out in these later Jewish teachers, and it was in a nation that to some extent, at least, was influenced by that teaching that Jesus was born.

Now in looking for a few moments at that figure which has fascinated so many hearts, round which the love and adoration of generation after generation of the Western world have twined, let us try to realize the work that He had to do, the mission He was intended to fulfil. A new civilization was to be born, a new departure in the life of the world; young nations, full of vigor, of energy, with the

[1] *Isaiah*, lviii. 4–8. [2] *Micah*, vi. 6–8.

metaphysical intellect less developed than the more practical side of the mind, were coming to the front, and were gradually to assume the reins of the destinies of the world. A strong and vigorous race, full of vitality, full of strength, full of practical ability, this was the type from which the nations of Europe were to be born—this was the nation, the race rather, whose religious training was the problem before the great Brotherhood, the guardians of the spiritual evolution of man. For that training another proclamation of the old truths was wanted; for the training and moulding of that new-dawning civilization again the old truths must be spoken by a messenger of that mighty Brotherhood. This also must be trained as others had been trained, and with a training suitable to its characteristics. Hence you find in Christianity comparatively little declaration by the Christ of subtle metaphysic, much of ethic, much noble morality, much spiritual teaching of a practical kind, little—in fact next to nothing—of the science of the soul. That was reserved for the esoteric teaching, confined to His immediate disciples. Looking as it were, over the district in which this religion was to begin, for a fit instrument and messenger of the Brotherhood, They chose one—a young man already marked out by a marvellous purity and by a profound devotion, Jesus, known later as the Christ. His mission began at that point of His life described in the gospels as His baptism, when He was about the age of thirty. At that period, as you may read in the gospels, the Spirit of

God came down upon Him, and he was proclaimed by a voice from heaven as the Son of God, to whom people were to listen.[1] On that phrase, "Son of God," I shall speak in a moment, when we come to deal with the challenge of the Jews to His claim to that position. It is enough for us to recognize that, according to the view put forward in the story of His life, His ministry begun when He was thirty years of age, when this special manifestation took place. From the occult standpoint, that is the allegorical way in which the choosing of this young man to be the messenger of the divine teaching is described, and represents the giving to Him of the illumination which made Him fit to be a divine Teacher of men. For three years only He led a teacher's life, a life beautiful in its purity, radiant with love, with compassion, with all the tenderest qualities of the human heart. We see Him wandering over the land of Palestine, raising the dead (as they were called), healing the sick, opening the eyes of the blind: miracles, men call these healings. But there is in them nothing surprising to the occultist, for he is familiar with such actions, he knows the powers by which they are done. For never yet has a great Teacher come to earth, one in whom the power of the Spirit was developed, who was not a master over physical nature, nature being subject to him and obedient to his will. These so-called miracles are nothing but the use of certain hidden powers of nature to bring about certain external re-

[1] *S. Matthew*, iii. 16, 17.

sults; these miracles of healing, of restoring the sight of the blind, and so on, were worked both long before the Christ was born, and have been repeated by many, years upon years afterwards, and so lightly did the Christ Himself hold them that when He spoke of them to His disciples He said: "Greater works than these shall ye do, because I go unto my Father."[1] He left it as the mark of the men who had real faith, living faith, in Him, that they should be able to take up serpents, and to drink poison without injury[2]—a mark belonging to all Initiates who choose to exercise the power, and the absence of which, at least in some sections of the Church, shows that they have lost that living faith of which their own Master laid down these powers as the outward symbol and expression.

The life of Jesus, as I said, is a beautiful life. Listen to His teachings, and there you will get His spirit, so different, alas! from the spirit which is often shown by those who bear His name. These teachings are exactly at one with the precepts of the great spiritual teachers who preceded him. "Blessed are the pure in heart; for they shall see God."[3] There is the occult truth which He again proclaimed, that only by purity can the Pure be seen, only by the purified can God be known. See how He enforces the teaching familiar to you, that thought is more important than action, that thought when it is performed is action practically done. "Whosoever,"

[1] *S. John*, xiv. 12. [2] *S. Mark*, xvi. 17, 18.
[3] *S. Matthew*, v. 8.

He said, "looketh on a woman to lust after her, hath committed adultery with her already in his heart."[1] Take again that teaching so familiar in the teaching of Manu, Zoroaster, and the Buddha: "Love your enemies, bless them that curse you, do good to them that hate you, and pray for them that despitefully use you and persecute you; that ye may be the children of your Father which is in heaven; for He maketh his sun to rise on the evil and on the good, and sendeth rain on the just and on the unjust."[2] See the occult statement, which probably few but occultists will understand: "The light of the body is the eye; if therefore thine eye be single, thy whole body shall be full of light; but if thine eye be evil, thy whole body shall be full of darkness. If therefore the light that is in thee be darkness, how great is that darkness."[3]

Listen to His proclamation once more of that ancient narrow path—the path that you know as sharp as the edge of the razor—"Strait is the gate, and narrow is the way which leadeth unto life, and few there be that find it."[4] Hear His words to the multitude, breathing out that divine compassion, which is the very birthmark of every one who comes from the great Brotherhood, from the great White Lodge: "Come unto me, all ye that labor, and are heavy laden, and I will give you rest. Take my yoke upon you, and learn of me, for I am meek and lowly in heart, and ye shall find rest unto your souls. For

[1] *Ibid.*, 28.
[2] *Ibid.*, 44, 45.
[3] *Ibid.*, vi. 22, 23.
[4] *Ibid.*, vii. 14.

my yoke is easy, and my burden is light."[1] See Him checking the disciples, as they tried to push away the mothers who brought their children to Him that He might bless them: "Suffer little children and forbid them not to come unto me, for of such is the kingdom of heaven."[2] And once He took a little child and set him in the midst as an example to His disciples of humility and submission. Take this sterner teaching, exactly again on the line of the ancient occult teaching, which says that attachment to the things of the earth is fatal to progress in the life of the spirit. When a young man goes to Him and asks how eternal life may be won, His first answer is the exoteric answer: "Keep the commandments." The answer of the young man is: "All these things have I kept from my youth up: what lack I yet?" Then comes the sterner demand: "If thou will be perfect, go and sell that thou hast, and give to the poor, and thou shalt have treasure in heaven; and come and follow me." The young man "went away sorrowful, for he had great possessions." And then the occult Teacher enforces the teaching on His disciples: "A rich man shall hardly enter into the kingdom of heaven. . . . It is easier for a camel to go through the eye of a needle, than for a rich man to enter into the kingdom of heaven."[3]

In this way then he taught the same ancient morality, the teaching so familiar to us all, the teaching of the ancient Founders of all religions. We trace another likeness to His predecessors in the teaching

[1] *Ibid.*, xi., 28–30. [2] *Ibid.*, xix. 14. [3] *Ibid.*, xix. 16–24.

by parables; always a parable was on His lips when He was speaking to the multitude. Parable after parable He spake, each one containing some gem of spiritual truth. Perhaps the one that has most held the heart of Christendom, and to which men's hearts have ever since answered because of its beauty and its tenderness, is that of the lost sheep, lost in the wilderness, for which the shepherd goes out and searches diligently till he finds it; "And when he hath found it, he layeth it on his shoulders, rejoicing. And when he cometh home, he calleth together his friends and neighbors, saying unto them, Rejoice with me; for I have found my sheep which was lost. I say unto you that likewise joy shall be in heaven over one sinner that repenteth, more than over ninety and nine just persons, which need no repentance."[1] The "Good Shepherd" is one of the favorite names of Christ throughout Christendom, and you may see Him in pictures, you may see Him in the painted windows of churches and cathedrals, drawn as "the Good Shepherd," with the lost lamb on His shoulder, which He has found and is bringing home rejoicing to the fold where the other sheep are kept. His doctrine of the "Kingdom of God" has been much perverted, but was well understood in the early Church; it was a kingdom into which men were invited, and in which the stages were clearly marked. Men must be pure ere they were allowed to enter; they must have faith; that is a necessity, ere they can come into it; they must

[1] *S. Luke*, xv. 3-7.

add to their faith knowledge, otherwise they cannot reach its higher grades; wisdom must follow knowledge, otherwise they remain imperfect; to all such immortality was promised—the conquest over death, the going out no more; for as we shall see presently, the Christian Religion in the early days taught the ancient doctrine of Reincarnation; hence there came a time when death was overcome and men went out no more from the Temple of God, when they had become perfect masters of the mysteries of the kingdom of heaven. Thus in teaching, in healing, in helping all who were in need, Jesus passed three brief years. He "went about doing good," is the summary of His life given by St. Peter.[1] Very short was His life, and why?

Because of the people to whom he came to bring the message of the Brotherhood: going to such a people, fierce, fanatical, harsh, and bigoted in their own religion, there could be but one result—the putting into action of their stern law of blasphemy, His slaying by hatred and by malice. Sometimes men ask to-day, why do the Masters remain hidden, why do They stay behind the veil and refuse to show Themselves in the haunts of men? Because until men relearn the ancient veneration, which made the messenger of the Gods a sacred person, and surrounded Him with love, with reverence, with worship, the Masters of Wisdom come not forth to stimulate the angry passions of men by jealousy of Their purity, by hatred of Their spiritual lives; the Christ was the

[1] *Acts*, xx. 38.

last of these great messengers sent to the world, and they to whom He came slew Him when three years of public life were over; they hated Him for a purity that seemed to them as an insult offered to their own impurity, and for a greatness that was a reproach to their littleness.

We now come to the struggles of the early Church. The gospel of love and of compassion spread swiftly amongst the poor, more slowly amongst the highly educated, by means of esoteric teaching; and we see a great effort made by the Brotherhood during the first three centuries after Christ. There was a struggle between learning and ignorance, a struggle between knowledge and superstition. It raged strongly and fiercely, having for its chief centre Alexandria, for its combatants the Gnostics on one side, the mass of Christians on the other. As you trace the story you find great Gnostic teachers, endeavoring to introduce the wisdom of the East under new names into this latest religion, intended for its modern vessel. The great Valentinus wrote his apocalypse of wisdom, the *Pistis Sophia*, the greatest treasure of ancient Christian occultism, now made known to the English-speaking world by the translation of Mr. G. R. S. Mead, the Secretary of the European Section of the Theosophical Society. Mr. Mead writes in his Introduction: "Let us then consider the movement about the year 150 A.D. By that time the original Logia or the Urevangelium of Christianity had disappeared, and the Synoptic Gospels were all set in the framework of the traditional life of the great Master of the Faith. The popular tidal wave of the new religion had come exclusively from the ocean of Jewish tradition, and was ingulfing a more universal view of Christianity in the same flood of intolerance and exclusiveness which had characterized the Hebrew nation throughout the whole of its previous history. This startling phenomenon was now attracting the attention of minds which were not only skilled in the philosophy of the schools, but also imbued with the eclectic spirit of a universal theosophy and a knowledge of the inner doctrines of the ancient religions. Such men thought that they saw in the Christian Gospel a similarity of doctrine and a universalism which was consanguineous with these inner teachings of the ancient faiths, and set to work to endeavor to check the exclusive and narrowing tendencies which they saw so rapidly developing among the less instructed, who made faith superior to knowledge, even to such an extent as to openly condemn every other form of religion, and scoff at all philosophy and education."[1]

The struggle raged between these men and the masses, led indeed by some wise and deeply instructed men, and it ended in the success of the unlearned multitude and in the casting out of the Church of the more learned and more philosophical Gnostics, who have ever since remained under the ban of heresy. The Church emerged from this struggle with enough of true religion left for train-

[1] *Pistis Sophia*, p. xxiii.

ing and elevating the heart, but not enough for justifying to the intellect the wisdom of the ages. It brought out of the struggle its devotion to the personal Christ, the man-God who was the object of its most passionate and most fervent worship. In that revelation of the Divine, there was, as I say, everything that was wanted for the heart; alas! there was not enough for the subjugation of the intellect, for the training of the philosophic mind. The result was that the Dark Ages came down upon Europe, the Dark Ages as they are rightly and fitly called in history, and the esoteric knowledge of the early Church disappeared; the fathers even were well-nigh forgotten, save in the monasteries, where they still were studied, and hence now and then the Roman Catholic Church gave doctors and metaphysicians to the world.

We can see how, during this time of darkness, doctrines were twisted and distorted, and how some of them became revolting alike to reason and to con science in the form in which they were presented. We come down to the time of the Protestant Reformation, when the terrible views of Calvin and the slightly more liberal views of Luther dominated the reforming party, and from them was evolved modern Protestantism, in its least crude form in the Church of England, ever largely influenced by Roman Catholic doctrines. Now, within the bosom of this Church itself, a nobler school is growing up, more liberal in its thinking, more charitable in its views of others, and we may hope that this will redeem later Christianity, and give it its rightful place amongst the religions of the world.

We must pass from this to the doctrines of Christianity and glance at them as fully as our time admits. The Trinity—of that there is curiously little said in the *Bible;* in the *Old Testament* there is nothing at all, although the Jews had the doctrine in their secret teaching, the Kabalah; in the *New Testament* there is little said of it, and the most precise statement is challenged—or rather is omitted—by the latest revisers of the *Bible*. This statement is very definite: "There are three that bear record in Heaven,—the Father, the Word, and the Holy Ghost: and these three are One."[1] The Revisers regarded this as a monkish gloss that had crept into the book later in the history of the Christian Church, and omitted it. That is the only text on which the doctrine can absolutely rely. There is a phrase at the end of the Gospel of S. Matthew as to baptism "in the name of the Father, and of the Son, and of the Holy Ghost," but that also has been challenged by criticism, though not rejected by the Revisers. There was in the early Church a struggle over the doctrine, which is complicated by the deification of Jesus into the Second Person, but ultimately it emerged from the struggle in a form recognizable as the ancient doctrine: the Father, existence, the source of all life; the Son begotten by, emanated from, Him, dual in His nature, God and man—with that mark of duality which is always the mark of the

[1] *S. John*, v. 7, old version.

second Logos or the second Person in the Trinity—by whom the worlds were made, and without whom nothing can be made in the manifested universe; more indefinitely the Third Person—the Holy Spirit, the Universal Mind, or Wisdom. As I say, there was a struggle in the Church. Some contested the doctrine of the Trinity; others maintained it; and finally the ancient doctrine emerged triumphantly from the struggle and became the orthodox doctrine of the Church. It was then authoritatively declared in the "Athanasian Creed," and, despite some of its clauses which are objectionable, that creed gives one of the best expositions of the metaphysic of the doctrine which is extant in Christianity. I recall it because there is dimly and vaguely suggested in it something behind the Trinity, also hinted at here and there in the course of the Christian Scriptures. The Divine Substance is said to be one. Believers are warned that as they must not confound the Persons of the Trinity, so neither must they divide the Substance, the unity which underlies the Three, the unity of which the Three are only the manifestations. A Roman Catholic theologian points out that the word Person comes from *persona*, a "mask"; and this must imply that behind the mask there is the unrevealed Reality, the hidden God, who is not known. There is a suggestion of this Unknown in the verse in Job: "Canst thou by searching find out God?"[1] More than once in the book of Job this question is suggested of the Unknowable, the unre-

[1] *Job*, xi. 7.

vealed God, unrevealed in His nature and in His essence. Then, coming downwards from the Trinity. we have the seven Spirits before the throne of God.[1] These are the seven great Gods of the Elements, familiar to us in Hinduism so far as five of them are concerned—the five Gods of the five manifested elements; here the whole seven are mentioned. Then we have, as lower Gods, all the Archangels and Angels, those of whom St. Paul speaks as angels, principalities, and powers;[2] of these there are nine orders: Seraphim, Cherubim, Thrones, Dominations, Virtues, Powers, Principalities, Archangels, and Angels. Very interesting in this connection is the statement of S. Ignatius, a bishop of the Apostolic Church, that he was not yet "able to understand heavenly things; as the places of the angels and the several companies of them, under their respective princes."[3] In the Roman Catholic Church there is, quite rightly, the worship of Angels, the worship, that is, of the lower Gods, who have to do immediately with man and with all the manifestations of nature.

Coming next to the important question of man's nature and of his relation to God, let us take it as taught in the Scriptures themselves, unhappily not always found in the teachings of the modern Church. S. Paul describes man as triple in his nature—spirit, soul, and body,[4] a distinction being made between spirit and soul that has dropped out of popular teach-

[1] *Revelation*, iv. 5. [2] *Romans*, viii. 38. [3] *Trallians*, 5.
[4] 1 *Thessalonians*, v. 23.

ing altogether, wherein the spirit and soul are identified, and so the whole of the evolution of man is confused. The spirit is divine; "Know ye not," said St. Paul, "that ye are the temple of God, and that the spirit of God dwelleth in you?"[1] Exactly the same form of words is here used with which we are so familiar in Hindu literature, where we find the human body spoken of as Vishnupûra, Brahmapûra—the town or city of Brahma or of Vishnu. Here S. Paul, himself an Initiate, speaks of the human body as God's temple, of the spirit of God as dwelling within it. And then—this is the passage that I had in my mind when I said I would allude to the Sonship of Christ which was proclaimed at His baptism—I find the Jews assailing Jesus because He claimed to be the Son of God; His defence is a remarkable one: He does not say, as a modern Christian might say of Him, "Yes, I am the Son of God, as no other man can be;" on the contrary He founds his claim to divine Sonship on the divinity which is inherent in the nature of man himself. Listen to His words, and see how clear, how definite they are. He refers the Jews to their own Scriptures. "Is it not written in your law, I said, ye are Gods? If he called them Gods unto whom the word of God came, and the Scriptures cannot be broken; say ye of him whom the Father hath sanctified and sent into the world, thou blasphemest; because I said, I am the Son of God?"[2] There is Christ's own defence of His Sonship: "All men are Gods, according to the Scrip-

[1] *Corinthians*, iii. 16. [2] *S. John*, x. 34-36.

tures, and the Scriptures cannot be broken: therefore there is no blasphemy in my claim, when I call myself also the Son of God." Then take that beautiful prayer just ere he goes to His crucifixion. He is praying to His Father about the future of His Church. He speaks to God of Their unity, that He is one with Him, and He goes on to pray that "they all may be one; as thou, Father, art in me and I in Thee, that they also may be one in us; . . . I in them and thou in me, that they may be made perfect in one."[1] There is the declaration of the unity of man with God. There is the proclamation in this religion also of man's divine nature, and of his reunion with the Father from whom for the time he seems to be separated, when dwelling in the body of flesh. If we take further the teaching as we find it in the writings of S. Paul this becomes clearer and clearer as we go on: for we find him using the term "Christ" as a mystic name for the principle of soul developing in man, the son of the father (spirit): "My little children, of whom I travail in birth again until Christ be formed in you."[2] Christ is not only to be a man external to His followers. He is to be formed as the babe within the womb in the heart of every one of His disciples. And this Christ who is to be born in the disciple is to grow, is to develop within him, until at last the man has attained unto "the measure of the stature of the fulness of Christ."[3] They are to become manifested Gods,

[1] *S. John*, xvii. 21, 23. [2] *Galatians*, iv. 19.
[3] *Ephesians*, iv. 13.

they are to become Gods manifest in the flesh. That is the teaching of apostolic Christianity, so sadly mutilated in its presentation by modern writers. And it is taught that all things are to be finally merged in God. Do you suppose that the teaching of union with, of merging in, Brahman is a teaching which Christianity had not? Then turn to the fifteenth chapter of the *Epistle to the Corinthians* and read the description that there is given: "Then cometh the end, when he shall have delivered up the kingdom to God, even the Father. . . . The last enemy that shall be destroyed is death . . . when all things shall be subdued unto him, then shall the Son also himself be subject unto him that put all things under him, that God may be all in all."[1] Just the old teaching coming out again, "God all in all," as the last stage of the universe; the Son, the Christ, gathering up all into Himself as Ishvara, and merging into Brahman, when God is all in all.

Let us next turn to reincarnation; that very verse just quoted, that the "last enemy that shall be destroyed is death," in itself gives a hint as to the teaching of the early Church, for death is said not to be destroyed till "the end." So also is a hint in the words: "Him that overcometh will I make a pillar in the temple of my God; and he shall go no more out,"[2] the going out being the going to rebirth, the exile from the heavenly places. But there are three cases which mark the doctrine more strongly so far as the Christ is concerned. It must be re-

[1] I *Corinthians*, xv. 24–28. [2] *Revelation*, iii. 12.

membered that belief in reincarnation was current among the Jews of His time, so that naturally references to it would be intelligible to all those about Him. But this fact is not enough to show that He accepted the doctrine. So take His words when some disciples came from John the Baptist and asked Him if He were the Christ. When the messengers had received His answer for their master, Jesus spoke of the character of the great preacher, and declared: "If ye will receive it, this is Elias which was for to come"[1]—a very clear statement that the Jewish prophet had reincarnated in John the Baptist. Again, when His disciples asked why it was said that Elijah would come before the Messiah, His answer was: "Elias truly shall first come and restore all things. But I say unto you that Elias is come already, and they knew him not. . . Then the disciples understood that he spake to them of John the Baptist."[2]

Again, His disciples asked Him about a blind man: "Who did sin, this man, or his parents, that he was born blind?" Now a modern Christian would answer: "How could a man have committed sin before he was born, so as to bring upon him this penalty?" But Jesus made no such ignorant reply. His reply was: "Neither hath this man sinned, nor his parents, but that the works of God should be made manifest in him."[3] He accepted the pre-existence of the soul and the possibility of sin com-

[1] *S. Matthew*, xi. 14. [2] *Ibid.*, xvii. 10–13.

[3] *S. John*, ix. 2, 3.

mitted before the present birth, but gave another reason for the blindness.

Turning to the fathers, we find that Tertullian speaks very plainly in his *Apology*. "If a Christian promises the return of a man from a man, and the very actual Gaius from Gaius, the cry of the people will be to have him stoned; they will not even so much as grant him a hearing. If there is any ground for the moving to and fro of human souls into different bodies [of animals], why may they not return into the very substance they have left, setting forth what is greatlier worthy of belief, that a man will come back from a man, any given person from any given person, still retaining his humanity; as that the soul, with its qualities unchanged, may be restored to the same condition though not to the same framework . . . . you ask, shall we be always dying and rising up from death? If so the Lord of all things had appointed, you would have to submit. . . . [But the millennium comes as limit and] after this there is neither death nor repeated resurrections." Origen held the belief in the pre-existence of the soul and of its being born into a body consonant with its previous deeds. He says: "Is it not more in conformity with reason that every soul, for certain mysterious reasons (I speak now according to the opinions of Pythagoras, and Plato, and Empedocles, whom Celsus frequently names), is introduced into a body, and introduced according to its deserts and former actions?"[1] Many passages might be

[1] *Contra Celsum*, I.

quoted, all showing a belief in the pre-existence of the soul and of its "descent" to take birth here, and there is no doubt that this belief was very widely spread in the early Church, for at a general Council it was formally condemned and stamped as a heresy—a Council held after darkness had begun its reign. This decision, more than anything else, divorced Christianity from the other religions of the world, and led to the most disastrous consequences. For with the doctrine of Reincarnation went the doctrine of Karma, the two depending one upon the other, and when Reincarnation is no longer believed Karma can no longer be taught. It was taught in the early epistles with no lack of plainness: "Be not deceived; God is not mocked; for whatsoever a man soweth that shall he also reap."[1] But when Reincarnation went, these words became unintelligible, and then all sorts of schemes had to be invented, schemes of vicarious atonement and what not, in order that men might not reap the results of their own doings. But when any such scheme is put to you by a Christian, who tells you that by that way you can escape the consequences of your actions, answer him in the words of his own Scriptures; "Be not deceived; God is not mocked; for whatsoever a man soweth that shall he also reap."

A noble doctrine, the doctrine of the law of sacrifice, underlies the idea of the vicarious atonement, but it has been travestied in a way which leads to the most terrible blasphemy. The law of sacrifice

[1] *Galatians*, vi. 7.

which brings about the union of man with God, the law of sacrifice by which the worlds were made, and by which the worlds are living, that noble doctrine of antiquity is shown forth in primitive Christianity by the perfect sacrifice of the Christ to the will of God. But it comes out in mediæval Christianity in schemes which put the Son and the Father to opposition, as it were, the one to the other, and which shock all reverence, as well as outrage all reason, by bringing in all kinds of legal quibbles into the relationship between the Spirit of God and man.

With the loss of Reincarnation came into existence another doctrine, in which Christianity is unique—the doctrine of an eternal hell. Heaven and hell equally eternal became the outcome of one's short life here. A man born into the world with his character already marked upon him, with vicious or virtuous tendencies, as the case might be, brought with him from the womb and stamped upon him in the cradle, that man, by living twenty, forty, sixty, one hundred years, was to fix the whole of his eternal destiny and go either to heaven or hell forevermore. How terribly that doctrine worked in demoralizing the minds of men, in making them selfish, I will only quote one verse to show—a verse written by one of the gentlest, noblest, purest men of modern Christianity, John Keble, the author of *The Christian Year*. He had been so demoralized by this doctrine of an eternal hell, by the idea that heaven and hell must stand or fall together, that in *The Christian Year* he gave voice to a sentiment which seems to me shocking in its selfishness and immorality; he pleaded for the doctrine of eternal torture because without it the idea of the eternal heaven would lose one of its supports. If some men are not tortured forever, there is no proof that others will have eternal place in heaven. He says—I quote from memory, but give the gist correctly:

> "But where is then the stay of contrite hearts?
> Of old they leant on Thine eternal word;
> But with the sinner's fear their hope departs.
> Fast linked as thy great name to Thee, O Lord,
> That we should endless be, for joy or woe:
> But if the treasures of Thy wrath could waste,
> Thy lovers must their promised heaven forego."

But if it were true that life in heaven depends on the tortures of others in hell, I ask you whether any man, with the Christ-spirit in him, would not accept annihilation for himself rather than buy his immortality by the misery of uncounted millions in a hell that knows no ending? Happily, this is a doctrine almost of the past; Christian after Christian is giving it up; teacher after teacher is proclaiming the opposite; Canon Farrar, preaching in the pulpit of Westminster Abbey, proclaimed the doctrine of "eternal hope" as against the doctrine of eternal hell, and only narrow and uncultured minds, who by the lack of the imaginative faculty are not able to realize the horrors of hell, only these continue to teach it and to make it part of Christianity.

I must go swiftly over the question whether the science of the soul is taught in Christianity. In the

Roman Catholic Church it is taught to a great extent, but not in the Protestant. I cannot tell you about the Greek Church, for I have no first-hand acquaintance with it; so that I must confine myself to the statement that in the Roman Catholic Church occultism has been to some extent preserved, and there some occult knowledge and some occult powers are still to be found. For instance, in the monastic orders methods of meditation are taught with careful particularity; among the monks and nuns of the contemplative orders there is a system of meditation that carries on the soul from step to step, from the first effort of imagination to the passing of the consciousness into the scene which is depicted; here is a remnant of the science of the soul, based upon a knowledge of facts. There are other occult traces in the Roman Catholic Church; the use of images, or idols, as Protestants call them, the use of holy water, of an ancient language—in which prayers were made by men of knowledge, the utility of prayer largely depending upon the sound which is produced. In these things are shown traces of the old teaching based on the understanding of the invisible world. Then there is the use of relics and of prayers for the dead—all signs of occult knowledge however fragmentary, however incomplete. And with what result? That they have produced mystics, saints, workers of "miracles," to an extent which the other sections of the Church cannot approach, and that you find among Roman Catholics mystics who speak of union with God and of the methods by which that union may be brought about on lines corresponding to the Hindu. Here again I cannot quote much, for the time is brief and the subject is long; but I may remind you of the exquisite *Imitation of Christ* by Thomas à Kempis, one of the most wonderful books ever produced by a Christian, a book that men of every faith might read with advantage. S. Thomas à Kempis gives instructions as to what a man must do if he would find Christ, and often the teaching is put into the mouth of Christ Himself. Take the teaching on the Self: "If man would find God he must learn," having left all things else, that "he leave also himself, and wholly go out of himself, and retain nothing of self-love."[1] A man ought "perfectly to forsake himself;"[2] "Son, leave thyself and thou shalt find me. . . . Lord, how often shall I resign myself, and in what things shall I leave myself?—always, and at all times, as in little, so also in great; I make no exception, but will have thee to be found in all things divested of thyself. Otherwise how canst thou be mine, and I thine, unless thou be both within and without freed from all self-will? . . . Aim only at this, pray for this, desire this, that thou mayest be divested of all self-seeking; and thus, naked, follow thy naked Jesus."[3] "A man's true progress consists in denying himself; and the man that has renounced himself is very much at liberty and very safe."[4] A Vedântin might have written: "Whatsoever is not God is

[1] *Op. cit.*, II. xi.
[2] *Ibid.*, III. xxxi.
[3] *Ibid.*, xxxvii.
[4] *Ibid.*, xxxix.

nothing, and ought to be accounted as *nothing*.[1] A man is not to be swayed by emotions, for great delight in devotion does not prove progress, but rather is it seen "in offering thyself with thy whole heart to the will of God . . . so that with the same equal countenance thou continue giving thanks, both in prosperity and adversity, weighing all things in an equal balance."[2] A pithy wisdom is found, also, that reminds one of the directness of the Buddha: "Where shall we find a man that is willing to serve God *gratis?*"[3] "What a man cannot mend in himself and others, he must bear with patience . . . . endeavor to be patient in supporting the defects and infirmities of others, of what kind soever; because thou also hast many things which others must bear withal. If thou canst not make thyself such a one as thou wouldst, how canst thou expect to have another according to thy liking?"[4] I might mention many others, but I have no time. I have gone beyond my lawful time in my desire to make you understand something of the religion which I know is too often travestied in your minds by the narrow interpretations which are continually put upon it.

And my appeal to Christians as to men of other religions would be an appeal for unity, for the breaking down of divisions; why should they not come on a common platform with all the rest of the great religions of the world? Why should not this young religion, with only eighteen centuries of life

[1] *Ibid.*, xxxi.
[2] *Ibid.*, xxv.
[3] *Ibid.*, II. xi.
[4] *Ibid.*, I. xvi.

behind it, come and join with Buddhism with its two thousand four hundred years of existence; with Zoroastrianism and with Hinduism, with their ten thousands and twenty thousands of years rolling backward into the past? Can they not see how they blaspheme God, when they declare that He has kept Himself for only one religion amongst all religions, and that wellnigh the youngest of them all? Can they not see how they outrage the Supreme, when they claim a unique platform, pushing all the rest of His children out into the darkness unrecognized by the Father of all spirits? Is not God called the Father of all spirits, and not only of the spirits incarnated in Christian bodies? If this unity could be gained all proselytism would cease; no man would try to convert another to his faith, but would rather try to learn what that other may have to teach him, what other views of God. For we can all learn from each other, Hindu from Christian, and Christian from Hindu; Zoroastrian from Buddhist, and Buddhist from Zoroastrian. Every religion is but one colored ray of the light of God, and in the union of all the religions the true white light is seen. As long as we separate ourselves we are colored by a particular ray. Let us study all religions, and love them all, and we shall then come nearer to the Fount in which we all have our origin and our ending.

You know well enough that I belong not to the religion that I here have been depicting; you know well enough that though born in it I was driven out of it by a narrow presentation, and knew not these truer and deeper views of that faith. But I say to you that all these religions come from one source. Their children should live as brothers and not as enemies, and none should try to convert others; all should be treated with respect. Hatred is of evil, in whatever religion it may be found. Let each man teach his own faith to those who desire to embrace it; let every man be free to speak of his views of God to all who are willing to listen to him. We are but facets of the Eternal; our poor intellects are narrow channels through which the life and love of God pour forth. Let us be channels in our own persons, but let us not deny that others are channels as much as we are, and that the divine life and love flow through them as well as through us. Then shall come peace wherein division shall arise not; then shall come unity, the harmony which is greater than identity. When His children live in love, then they may hope to know something of the love of God, for truly spake a Christian teacher: "He that loveth not his brother whom he hath seen, how can he love God whom he hath not seen?"[1]

[1] 1 *S. John*, iv. 20.